CORNELIUS O'KEEFE

AMAZING STORIES

CORNELIUS O'KEEFE

The Life, Loves, and Legacy of an Okanagan Rancher

SHERRI FIELD

HERITAGE

VICTORIA · VANCOUVER · CALGARY

Copyright © 2019 Sherri Field
Foreword copyright © 2019 Ken Mather

All rights reserved. No part of this publication may be reproduced, stored in a retrieval system, or transmitted in any form or by any means—electronic, mechanical, audio recording, or otherwise—without the written permission of the publisher or a licence from Access Copyright, Toronto, Canada.

Heritage House Publishing Company Ltd.
heritagehouse.ca

*Cataloguing information available from
Library and Archives Canada*

978-1-77203-248-2 (pbk)
978-1-77203-249-9 (epub)

Edited by Hayley Evans
Proofread by Stephen Harries
Cover photo courtesy of the Vernon Museum and Archives

The interior of this book was produced on 100% post-consumer recycled paper, processed chlorine free, and printed with vegetable-based inks.

We acknowledge the financial support of the Government of Canada through the Canada Book Fund (CBF) and the Canada Council for the Arts, and the Province of British Columbia through the British Columbia Arts Council and the Book Publishing Tax Credit.

23 22 21 20 19   1 2 3 4 5

Printed in Canada

*To all the local pioneers whose hard work
helped make the Okanagan Valley what it is today,
and to all those people who are working
to preserve their legacies.*

Contents

FOREWORD 1
INTRODUCTION 3
CHAPTER 1   A Pioneering Spirit. 6
CHAPTER 2   Humble Beginnings 9
CHAPTER 3   Go West, Young Man, Go West! 25
CHAPTER 4   Birth of a Ranching Empire. 32
CHAPTER 5   The Rancher Finds a Wife 41
CHAPTER 6   Land Disputes. 46
CHAPTER 7   More Wealth, More Prestige 52
CHAPTER 8   Additions, Achievements, and Accolades . . . 62
CHAPTER 9   Cattle Baron to Land Baron. 69
CHAPTER 10 Marriage, Mining, and Milling 98
CHAPTER 11 Technology and Other Amenities. 107
CHAPTER 12 The Beginning of the End 112
CHAPTER 13 The Legacy. 115
ACKNOWLEDGEMENTS 120
NOTES 123
BIBLIOGRAPHY. 137
INDEX. 145

Foreword

CORNELIUS O'KEEFE HAS long been recognized as one of the first ranchers in British Columbia's Okanagan Valley. After pre-empting 65 hectares in 1867, he eventually amassed over 4,856 hectares of land in the North Okanagan. His ranch—which became the BC Express stagecoach depot at the end of the wagon road from Fort Kamloops to the Okanagan—was the home of the Okanagan's first general store and post office, with O'Keefe as the first postmaster. O'Keefe's entrepreneurial spirit led him to diversify his agricultural activities by raising sheep, growing wheat, and in the early 1890s, planting one of the first orchards in the valley. He also constructed a grist mill and later was a major investor in the Okanagan Flouring Mills Company in nearby Armstrong. With the completion of the Canadian Pacific Railway in 1885, O'Keefe took his place among the leaders of the settler community in the North Okanagan, with his magnificent Queen Anne-style mansion constructed in 1886 as a symbol of his success.

O'Keefe remained active in the community, and in 1907, he sold the majority of his land to a Belgian consortium: the Land and Agricultural Company of Canada. With this purchase, much of the land in the North Okanagan was opened up for settlement and orchard development, and a new era began in the region. This purchase enabled O'Keefe to continue ranching on a small scale and to construct theatres in Vernon and Kamloops. A justice of the peace, he also served as the director of the British Columbia Cattle Association, director of the Okanagan and Spallumcheen Agricultural Society, and president of the Vernon Jockey Club. He was active in the Conservative Party, and in 1911 he was elected as the honorary president of the Vernon Conservative Association. He lived until his death in 1919 in his lovely ranch house, which remained in the family's hands until 1977 and is preserved today as a historic site.

Sherri Field has conducted extensive research for years on this fascinating individual and has uncovered much new information on his humble origins and early life. Her account helps us to better understand his complex and commanding personality, and this book is recommended to anyone who has visited the Historic O'Keefe Ranch or just wants to know more about the Ranch's founder and its history.

—Ken Mather, Curator Emeritus
Historic O'Keefe Ranch

Introduction

I FIRST VISITED the Historic O'Keefe Ranch in 1967, when I was twelve, the year the Ranch opened. The antiques in the mansion sparked my imagination, and I have been back many times since, as a visitor, a researcher, and a heritage interpreter. When I pursued an undergraduate degree as a mature student in the mid-1990s, one course was on the history of BC with Dr. Duane Thomson, and it seemed natural to turn to the Ranch and Cornelius O'Keefe for the subject of a research paper. Dr. Thomson encouraged me to pursue the topic further in a directed study with him. He saw its potential for publication, prompting me to look more fully into the life of O'Keefe, to the point of taking two research trips to Ottawa.

This book details O'Keefe's journey as a son of poor parents to being a wealthy "Father of the Okanagan." His life deserves

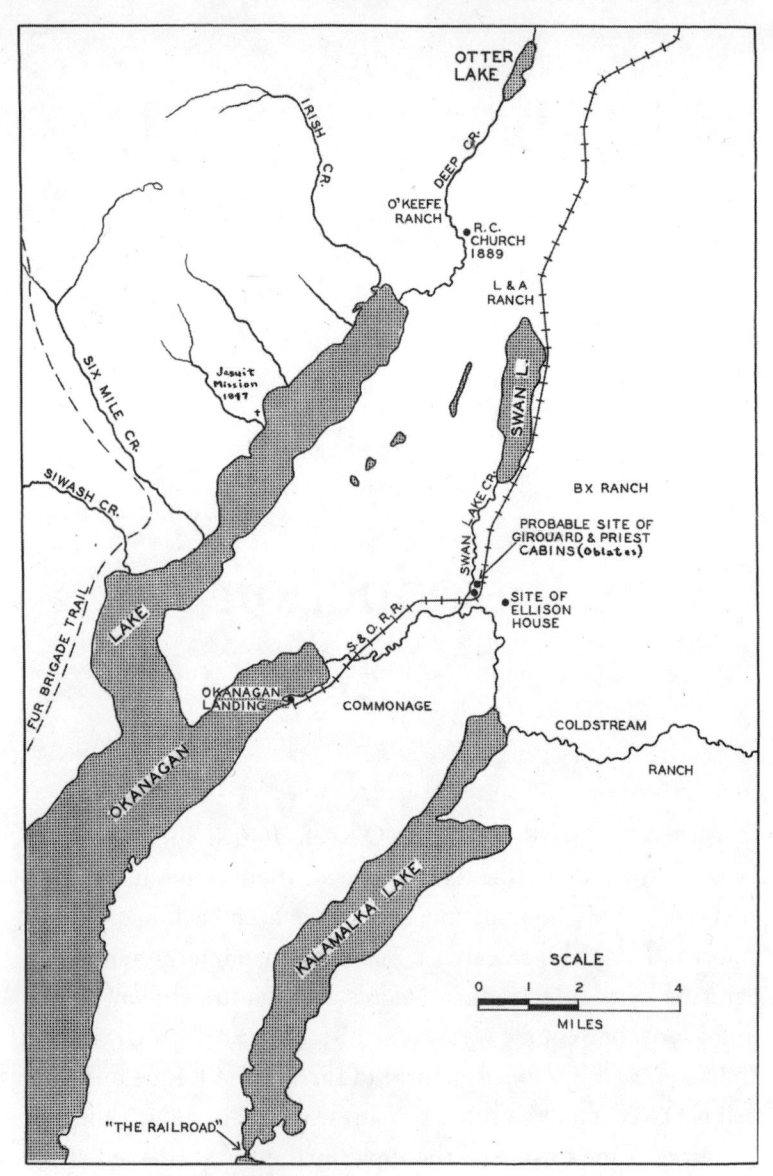

This map, ca. 1896, shows the location of Cornelius O'Keefe's ranch on Deep Creek, at the head of Okanagan Lake, in relation to other local ranches, including the BX and Coldstream. It also shows the route of the Shuswap & Okanagan Railroad (the S & O) and its proximity to some of O'Keefe's grazing lands.
COURTESY OF VERNON MUSEUM AND ARCHIVES

Introduction

recording. The earliest history written on the subject is by Thomas Leo O'Keefe, a son from Cornelius O'Keefe's first white family. His unpublished manuscript, "The Exploits and Adventures of Cornelius O'Keefe," penned prior to 1977, is based on his own recollections of life on the ranch, but he concludes his narrative at 1900, the year his mother, Mary Ann, died. Edna Oram, a former ranch manager, wrote a short history in 1978, which cites only newspaper articles, and some of the information is erroneous. Shortly thereafter came Stan McLean's *The History of the O'Keefe Ranch*, published in 1984. McLean was a heritage interpreter at the ranch in 1979 and 1980 and was encouraged by the board of directors to write his own book when he questioned why there was no information on the ranch that was available to the public. While his book is more informative than either O'Keefe's or Oram's works, it focuses primarily on the twentieth-century operations of the Ranch and does not provide a strong background on the origins of Cornelius O'Keefe's cattle empire. The most recent publication is Ken Mather's *Home Sweet Home*, written in 1995. While the research is sound, it was intentionally limited, as it was written to sell in the Ranch gift shop as a souvenir catalogue and to showcase some of the most important artifacts in the Ranch's collection.

My book is based largely on primary sources: newspapers, census returns, and the O'Keefe Ranch files and archives, to name just a few. I include several family stories, because much of what we know, or think we know, comes from these anecdotes; some have become legends for Ranch staff and volunteers, and ultimately, for visitors. Some history has been obscured, or at least buried—until someone digs deeper.

CHAPTER

1

A Pioneering Spirit

Residents of this city and district were greatly shocked on Tuesday morning when it became known that Mr. Cornelius O'Keefe had died at his home near the Head of the Lake. Particularly among the old-timers of the Okanagan will this news be received with deep regret, as Mr. O'Keefe was a pioneer of the pioneers, and was one of the few remaining representatives of the men who broke into the wilderness of the Interior at a time when it was a land practically unknown to the outside world... Mr. O'Keefe was... among those who took part in the early rush to the goldfields of the Cariboo... When he... reached the Okanagan in 1867 there were few white settlers in the country... Mr. O'Keefe's activities were for many years linked up with the progress of the Okanagan. The original band of cattle which he brought in with him soon grew to large herds, and as the country opened up he became one of

A Pioneering Spirit

Cornelius O'Keefe, ca. 1905.
COURTESY OF THE HISTORIC O'KEEFE RANCH

the most progressive farmers. His broad acres made him one of the largest wheat growers in the province, and his industry and business ability soon brought him to a state of affluence.

VERNON NEWS, MAY 29, 1919

IN A GLOWING obituary in the *Vernon News*, we learn of the death of that "pioneer of the pioneers," Cornelius O'Keefe. The article about him that followed in the *Vernon News* elaborates on the pioneering spirit of the man who arrived in the Okanagan with nothing and died a wealthy man:

> Mr. O'Keefe was, like all his associates in that pioneer band who endured such hardships and privations in the days when trails were few and wagon roads, to say nothing of railways,

something undreampt [sic], a man of courage, foresight and fortitude. In addition he was possessed of business ability of no mean order and soon accumulated a valuable property. He was of untiring energy, and in his prime was a splendid type of the men who have blazed the trails along which civilization and progress found their way. His name is inseparably connected with the pioneer history of the Okanagan, and his death reminds one of how few are now left of that rapidly thinning band of adventurous spirits to whom the present generation owes more than most people realize.

How does a man rise above his very humble beginnings as the son of an illiterate immigrant farmer and become a highly respected cattle baron, land magnate, and forward-thinking entrepreneur? Such is the stuff of legend, and such is the story of one of the Okanagan's most well-known pioneers.

CHAPTER

2

Humble Beginnings

THE NINETEENTH CENTURY saw a huge expansion into Western Canada. The Cariboo Gold Rush was in full swing by 1860, and although it was virtually over by 1866, navigable roads into that area were still needed. The Corps of Royal Engineers were tasked with building "the 600-kilometre Cariboo Road from [Fort] Yale to the centre of the new gold rush at Barkerville,"[1] and tradesmen were needed to fulfill the various jobs necessary to the road-building process.

People moved to the colony known as British Columbia for many reasons, but they all had one thing in common: they wished to succeed in a new territory, whether it was by building roads, by farming, or by prospecting for gold. Many of these people left their homes in the east with only what they could carry, and they came from a multitude of ethnic and religious backgrounds, including English, Scottish, and Irish, Anglican, Presbyterian, and Catholic.

Being truly successful in the farming or ranching industry required not only knowledge of crops and animals, but also enough good land to support a viable operation. Those who had the foresight to take advantage of propitious times to purchase land and who knew the best means to acquire it, were often among the most prosperous. In addition, some people believed they had to work harder for their success because they were not part of an area's prevailing culture or religion. Sometimes unwittingly, they strove for social prominence by building fine homes and being among the first to incorporate new technology into them. The willingness to try new technology in the home was often also accompanied by a willingness to utilize new advances in farming technologies and practices.

It was this combination of knowledge about farming, the ability to predict real estate trends and settlement patterns, and a willingness to embrace new technology that often led to social and financial success. Such a person was Cornelius O'Keefe, who came from an Irish Catholic background in Ontario (where so many were English Protestants). He brought with him knowledge, foresight, and an inclination to accept new ideas. The life he created for himself in the West very much resembled that which he had left behind. Because of the knowledge and experience he had gained while working on the family farm in Ontario, O'Keefe was able to acquire huge tracts of land and build not one but two fine homes.

Humble Beginnings

* * *

Cornelius O'Keefe was born on July 26, 1837, in Fallowfield, near Ottawa, to Michael and Esther O'Keefe. He helped his father operate the family farm, and was well accustomed to hard work and poverty. His father was born in Ireland in 1782, while his wife, Esther, was born in Lower Canada in 1814.[2] In the *Répertoire des mariages de la cathédrale d'Ottawa*, Esther's French name is listed as Esthère Demers, which, when anglicized, became Esther Demara. She was probably from a lower-class family that was quite happy to marry her off to a hardworking Irish immigrant navvy, even though he was more than thirty years her senior.[3]

Michael O'Keefe probably arrived in Canada in 1819. As a poor, unskilled labourer, he came to Canada to work on the canals that joined the St. Lawrence River to the Great Lakes. These canals were begun in the 1820s to enable better transportation not only of goods, but also of military personnel. In the 1842 Census for Canada West—Carleton County, Michael indicated that he had been in Canada for twenty-three years. In 1829, he signed a petition stating that his experience in Canada was a positive one, and that he would encourage others to emigrate as well. O'Keefe's illiteracy was evident on the petition: he signed it with an X rather than an actual signature. The list of names on the petition was compiled from a questionnaire that was distributed "to the Irishmen working on the first sections of the Rideau Canal near the new village of Bytown," and who had immigrated under the Honourable Peter Robinson several years earlier. Although "there is no reason to think that all signers" to the petition were employed on the canal works, "in all likelihood the bulk of them were." Nevertheless, the inclusion of O'Keefe's name on this list proves that he was definitely in the country on February 5, 1829.[4]

By 1842, Michael O'Keefe held a deed for eighty hectares of land, of which twenty-four had been improved. The census shows that the O'Keefe family had farmed thirty bushels of wheat, one hundred of oats, four hundred of potatoes, ten of barley, five of Indian corn, and sixty-eight kilograms of maple syrup, and were in possession of eight cattle, five horses, nine sheep, and seven hogs. The survey also shows other products manufactured by the family, including eleven metres of fulled cloth, thirty-six metres of flannel or other woollen cloth (not fulled), and twenty-three kilograms of wool.[5]

Beginning in 1824, the British government sold one million hectares, at a total cost of £348,068, to the Canada Company.[6] The agreement with the British government stipulated that the Canada Company build roads to make the land accessible, thus enticing good settlers. The company also had to "pay so much a year to the Executive Council until payment [of the purchase amount] was completed." The Canada Company then began to sell the land to former canal workers. When the land proved too costly for many labourers to buy, the company implemented a plan to allow people to occupy land "at a rent of a shilling an acre."[7] Michael O'Keefe was one of those who acquired land through the Canada Company in 1851; by 1861, he controlled a further forty hectares of land in addition to that which he had previously settled.[8] The choice of land near Nepean in Carleton County was not a random one: in 1851, Nepean had five water-powered sawmills, a woollen mill, a grist mill, and a distillery, all of which gave the O'Keefe family access to the consumers of their farm's products.

Humble Beginnings

[T]he qualities of the soil in Carleton [County] is [sic] good, though there is, of course, much of its area which is of such a nature as to be entirely worthless. Most of this is of so extremely rocky a nature as to be incapable of sustaining vegetable growth.[9]

However, rocky soil notwithstanding, many crops were raised, including grain and vegetable crops in abundance and of excellent quality, the atlas tells us. Perhaps a further reason for settling near Nepean was the proximity of a Roman Catholic church, the first in the area outside the city of Ottawa, which provided the benefit of Catholic neighbours.

The Personal Census of 1861 indicates that the O'Keefe family owned a one-and-a-half-storey log house, for six children and their parents.[10] Between 1851 and 1861, the O'Keefes had sufficiently cleared fourteen hectares upon which they planted various crops. The clearing of this land was quite a feat, since the timbered areas were extremely dense, with several varieties of evergreen and deciduous trees, all of which had to be removed.[11] According to Harry and Olive Walker, in their book *Carleton Saga*, "land clearing was a laborious process of dragging out the tenacious stumps by oxen and later by a stump-puller... Potatoes planted among stumps were often the first staple crops in the struggle for survival."[12]

With their farming tools and implements valued at $50, the O'Keefes evidently possessed only the most rudimentary of tools with which to clear their land.[13] The task must have been a backbreaking one: cutting trees and underbrush with only an axe or two and pulling tree stumps using the family's single team of horses. Michael O'Keefe turned sixty-nine years old in 1851; he was probably physically unable to perform much heavy work any longer. No doubt much of the work done between that year and 1861 fell to his children, including the young Cornelius O'Keefe, who, at fourteen, was the seventh child and third son, and who would have been mature enough to assume the work of an adult man. The younger O'Keefe probably helped his father in building the family home, too, which included felling the trees on their own property. The house was made of logs; they did not need a sawmill to cut the logs into lumber. These experiences with land clearing, horse logging, and house building left the younger O'Keefe well prepared to endure the hard work needed to start a farm later in British Columbia.

In addition to their fourteen hectares of completely cleared land, the O'Keefes had eighteen hectares of pasture and an eight-hectare woodlot. Again, Cornelius O'Keefe likely undertook much of the work involved in gathering the family's fuel. He was also well versed in caring for animals, and with one steer or heifer, three milk cows, eight sheep, and four pigs, he would have had experience in milking, shearing, and butchering, as these animals likely provided most of the family's needs for dairy, wool, and meat.[14] Certainly, caring for the stock animals helped to make him largely self-sufficient. Making butter, as well as the cleaning, carding, spinning, and knitting of wool would have been the responsibilities of the female members of the family, while whole families were involved in the harvesting of grain, "which was cut with a cradle and collected into stooks by the settler's wife and children."[15] A cradle was a variation of the scythe; it resembled a webbed hand attached to the scythe's handle. Once cut, the cradle was tipped to allow the straw to be dropped onto a pile. Using this

Humble Beginnings

tool was easier on the back, as one did not have to bend over to cut. A skilled cradler could "cut two acres of wheat per day."[16]

Once the grain was cut, a settler needed to have it milled into flour, so he "carried his bag of wheat on his back over blazed trail—straining across muskeg, fording creeks, struggling over hardwood heights until he emerged in sight of a mill." While the men and boys did the difficult fieldwork, the women made lye soap using the household ashes. They also made candles and clothes, spun and dyed wool, milked cows, made butter and cheese, preserved pork by smoking and salting it, made pickles, and did all the cooking and baking. Truly, "it was the women who set the standard of home life in the wilderness."[17] Young Cornelius observed the way an effective household works and took these memories with him when he moved west and later married.

* * *

While the O'Keefes had what they needed to live, they were by no means rich. When the census was taken in 1861, the O'Keefes had only sixty-eight kilograms of butter and two ninety-kilogram barrels of pork put aside; this was slightly lower than the area's average of seventy-three kilograms of butter and three barrels of pork, so it seems that the family subsisted mainly on crops produced on the family farm.[18] They did not produce enough to sell for profit, and purchasing anything from other farmers would have been expensive. The O'Keefes also owned two horses, which they used for farm work such as ploughing and harvesting and for other tasks including logging and transportation. They also had one colt or filly that was too young to be used as a work animal. Unlike many of their neighbours, the O'Keefes did not possess a pleasure carriage, a conveyance that was not sturdy enough for use in farm work, and they could not afford a luxury buggy that had no use as a farm vehicle. They would have used the adult horses for riding and packing as well as for working the farm.

The O'Keefe family was quite poor compared with two neighbouring families: the McKennas and the Tierneys (Cornelius O'Keefe was to marry first a daughter of the McKennas and later a granddaughter of the Tierneys). O'Keefe's farm was valued at only $1,200 in 1861, while Charles McKenna's operation was valued at $3,000. Like the O'Keefes, McKenna held forty hectares in total, but his farming equipment, valued at $100, was worth twice that of O'Keefe's in 1861. With twenty-six of his forty hectares under crops in 1860, McKenna had planted almost twice the acreage planted by O'Keefe.[19] McKenna and his family lived in a one-and-a-half-storey stone house, a much more substantial structure than O'Keefe's log house.[20] O'Keefe had six hectares planted in wheat that produced 350 bushels in 1860, while McKenna had ten hectares in wheat that yielded 420 bushels.[21] O'Keefe also had seven hectares of oats that produced 450 bushels; McKenna had only five hectares of oats, but they produced 480 bushels. Between 1856 and 1860, the average price of one bushel of oats was thirty-five cents, while the same amount of wheat paid ninety-two cents.[22] Even if the O'Keefes had sold their entire 450-bushel crop of oats, they would have earned a total of only $157.50; however, they probably used the oats for feed and seed rather than as a cash crop, so they made little—if any—money from this particular crop. In addition, O'Keefe's 350 bushels of wheat were also needed for the family's own needs, so again, the family probably earned no money from its

Humble Beginnings

wheat crop, which meant that they maintained only a subsistence-level operation.

Each family had just under a hectare planted in potatoes, but while O'Keefe produced only two hundred bushels, McKenna produced three hundred; both men would have used the potatoes as a food crop for their animals. In addition, McKenna harvested 350 bushels of turnips from 0.2 hectares, while O'Keefe planted none. McKenna also had twenty tonnes of hay while O'Keefe had only fifteen, although McKenna needed more animal feed because he had more stock, including six young steers or heifers, five milk cows, ten sheep, five pigs, and two horses.[23] Although the cows and pigs probably provided enough produce to meet the family's needs, some of the sheep were likely sold for cash. This same year, the McKenna family had 180 kilograms of butter—more than twice that of the O'Keefes'—as well as five barrels of pork.[24]

Like O'Keefe, McKenna owned two horses that were used for farm work and transportation, but because he also owned a pleasure carriage, the horses would have been trained for driving as well as riding.[25] Why McKenna was better off financially is not clear from the census, but it is possible that he had occupied his land for a longer period of time. He definitely had more family help, because at eighteen and twenty years of age, his two oldest sons would have been of great help to their father. There was also a twelve-year-old son, and although he was in school for at least part of the year, he was old enough to do a certain amount of work on the farm during peak farming times. At forty-five years of age, McKenna was more than thirty years younger than O'Keefe and therefore much better able to perform the back-breaking work involved in running a farm. It is not surprising that McKenna was wealthier than O'Keefe.[26]

There is also evidence that the Tierney family was faring better than the O'Keefes. Denis Tierney (who would be the grandfather of Elizabeth, Cornelius O'Keefe's second wife) arrived in Canada around 1824, bringing with him several of his adult children from his first marriage (his first wife had died around 1820), as well as his second wife and their two children. Given that Tierney was able to afford ship passage for his entire family in the 1820s, and then to purchase land in Nepean, it is reasonable to conclude that he arrived in Canada well prepared to live in the wilderness. In 1842, Denis Tierney and Michael O'Keefe were more or less equals in terms of landholdings and farm production, but by 1861, Tierney had surpassed O'Keefe in both. Both Tierney and O'Keefe occupied eighty-one hectares of land in 1842, but the latter had improved twenty-four hectares, while the former had improved only fourteen.[27] In addition, each held the deed to his land. Each man had produced four hundred bushels of potatoes and one hundred bushels of oats in the previous year; O'Keefe had also raised five bushels of Indian corn and made sixty-eight kilograms of maple sugar, while Tierney had none of either. Perhaps the maple sugar production had less to do with the actual cultivation and more to do with fortuity; O'Keefe's land probably had sugar maple trees growing naturally, while Tierney's did not. However, O'Keefe had produced only thirty bushels of wheat compared to Tierney's one hundred, but he had also produced ten bushels of barley while Tierney had none.

In terms of livestock, O'Keefe had eight head of cattle compared to Tierney's seven, and each owned five horses. O'Keefe had

Humble Beginnings

nine sheep and seven hogs; Tierney had ten and six, respectively. The men also produced similar amounts of cloth: Tierney had made eighteen metres of flannel or other woollen cloth and O'Keefe had made thirteen, but Tierney had procured almost double the number of kilograms of wool (at fourteen) than O'Keefe had (at seven).

John Tierney, the eldest son of Denis Tierney, was fairly close in age to Michael O'Keefe. By 1842, John was well established; he owned forty hectares of land, of which fourteen were improved. The 1842 census indicates that John, who had been in Canada for eighteen years, had two hundred bushels of wheat, two hundred and fifty of oats, three hundred of potatoes, as well as eight cattle, three horses, twelve sheep, and six hogs. His family had produced eleven metres of fulled cloth, thirty-seven metres of flannel or other woollen cloth (not fulled), and twenty-three kilograms of wool. Although Michael O'Keefe owned more land than John Tierney, the O'Keefes produced considerably fewer bushels of produce than did the Tierneys.

By 1861, John Tierney held sixty hectares, with thirty-two under cultivation, of which twenty-four were planted in crops in 1860, more than either Michael O'Keefe or Charles McKenna. Like the McKennas, John Tierney's family lived in a one-and-a-half-storey stone house.[28] Tierney's farm had a cash value of $4,440, and he had $150 worth of farm equipment. He had ten hectares planted in wheat that yielded 600 bushels, as well as three hectares in peas, three in oats, approximately one in potatoes, and approximately one in turnips, which produced 160, 240, 400, and 800 bushels, respectively.[29]

Tierney would have kept part of his wheat crop to meet his family's needs, but it is likely that he sold the remainder. Similarly, although Tierney would have used a portion of his feed crops for his animals, he might have had enough to sell and therefore make a profit. He had a larger number of stock animals than did either O'Keefe or McKenna—another indication that Tierney was prospering. In addition to six milk cows, he had six steers or heifers, so he was engaged in increasing his herd naturally and perhaps had little need to buy new animals regularly. Tierney also owned three horses, four colts or fillies, ten sheep, and six pigs, some of which would have been used for his family while others may have been sold.

In 1860, Tierney put up 181 kilograms of butter and six barrels of pork, which he would have kept for the family's use, and like McKenna, Tierney owned a pleasure carriage, valued at $80. Like O'Keefe, Tierney had one son, eighteen years old, who could work on the farm, as well as a younger son, eleven, who had not attended school in 1860 and likely performed a share of the farm work. Because John Tierney was only fifty-six years old and had two sons capable of working full-time on the farm, he was perhaps better equipped physically to handle a larger operation than Michael O'Keefe.

Since Tierney was already relatively wealthy when he arrived in Canada, he was able to purchase most, if not all, necessities to sustain his farm and keep it productive. There were other signs of the Tierneys' wealth. For example, they owned a musk ox robe to keep them warm on the sleigh during the winter; the only other such robe in all of Ontario at the time, according to an O'Keefe family story, was owned by the then governor general of Canada.[30] In addition, John Tierney held the position of Nepean town collector for two years: 1852 and 1853. Neither Denis nor John Tierney

Humble Beginnings

needed to find other work off his farm to support his family, so neither would have worked on the canals where O'Keefe had worked.

***

Although the patriarchs of all three families were born in Ireland, only O'Keefe experienced the ethnic prejudice found along most of the canal works when he worked there during the 1820s and 1830s. As a youngster, Cornelius O'Keefe must have been aware of the ethnic problems faced primarily by Irish navvies, including his father; perhaps these early experiences with discrimination led the younger O'Keefe to seek a higher social position in life. The Irish canal workers were thought by the predominantly English population to be "irrational, emotionally unstable, and lacking in self-control"[31] and were known for their heavy drinking and fighting; violence "usually occurred when traditional ethnic, occupational, or geographic boundaries were crossed... [and] when the local gentry held a village fair at Bytown in 1829, brawling broke out between Irish workers and farmers [from] the surrounding area."[32] Along the canal was a small settlement

> with a number of "shebeens" or log taverns... [An] observant settler named Abraham Dow... kept a record of social happenings. One of these was a riot on St. Patrick's Day when 200 Bytown Irish marched to Hog's Back [a rapids along the canal] to celebrate the event with their compatriots... and they amused themselves by fighting.[33]

It seems that the Irish were somewhat notorious as brawlers. The suggestion is that the Irish actually enjoyed fighting; since many of them thought that "a fair was of little use unless a few heads were cracked," if a fight had not yet been started, one man would give "his neighbour, who was his best friend, a crack across the head with a stick, and the battle [would] commence."[34]

The workday for the average canal worker was fourteen to sixteen hours per day, six days a week;[35] the hard play seems to have balanced the hard work. Michael O'Keefe had likely told his children of his problems while working on the canal, and because he was Catholic as well as Irish, he may have experienced even more intolerance. Irish Catholic labourers were thought to be unreasonable and without self-control because they confronted employers and law enforcement officials, as well as local residents and each other.[36] Violence was not limited to the Rideau Canal works; it was reported along the Welland, Lachine, and Saint Lawrence Canals as well. Young Cornelius O'Keefe might very well have been subjected to a certain amount of ethnic prejudice and discrimination.

* * *

Cornelius's early education was rather extensive, considering the family's poverty. Because Michael O'Keefe was illiterate, he might have desired more education for his family; the proximity of the local school might have been an added incentive for him to enroll his children in classes. Indeed, as of 1847, Nepean had at least one school, and "the highest average paid [to teachers] by any municipality was by Nepean, [at] $392.20 [per annum] per teacher"; it is highly likely that young Cornelius received the best possible elementary education, given that the township attracted the best possible teachers with its high salary.[37] The 1851 Census of the Township of Nepean in Carleton County indicates that Cornelius attended school for at least part of that year, so he would have received instruction in mathematics, reading, and writing. He probably also spoke French fluently, since his mother was from Lower Canada; furthermore, because he was confirmed at St. Patrick's Catholic Church in Fallowfield, he would have received a religious education as well. As we will see, he maintained his ties to the Church throughout his life.

Young Cornelius O'Keefe must have been aware of the benefits of a railway in the area, and of having an affiliation with a local military organization. The railway connecting "Bytown" (which would later become Ottawa) and Prescott began operation in December 1854,[38] and he would have been aware of the financial benefits to be derived from it. Fallowfield was only a few kilometres from Bytown, so it was easy to transport crops or animals to the rail yards. Even though the O'Keefes may not have had much in the way of cash crops and therefore had little need for the railway, Cornelius O'Keefe knew that proximity to a rail yard could do much to increase the profitability of a farming operation and property values in general.

It is also probable that, before leaving home in 1861, young Cornelius was involved with the local militia; certainly, his father would have been enrolled in a company. The township of Nepean was second only to Bytown in terms of its size, wealth, and population.[39] Nepean probably had a militia company, since such "companies were... only formed in the larger towns [and] were mostly called Rifles."[40] It is reasonable to believe that the elder O'Keefe was enrolled because "under the Militia Act of 1793... each male inhabitant aged 16 to 50 was required to enroll his name as a militiaman and attend annual muster on the King's birthday,

4 June."[41] At forty-seven years of age, Michael O'Keefe was within the age limitations, although the county's first "organization of this description" was in approximately 1854.[42] Nepean's "geographical position" was "so advantageous... that the great military canal terminus [was located] within its north-east corner."[43] Cornelius O'Keefe's affiliation with a military organization would have given him the opportunity to realize the potential political benefits to be derived from his membership. Indeed, his 1887 provincial appointment as a justice of the peace in British Columbia is further evidence of his upward mobility.

CHAPTER

3

Go West, Young Man, Go West!

WHILE LITTLE IS known about Cornelius O'Keefe between 1861, when he left his family's home, and 1867, when he founded his ranch in British Columbia, it is probable that he had heard of the gold strikes of 1858 and went west to make his fortune. Still, what would possess him to leave his family and everything he knew and travel to an essentially unsettled area several thousand kilometres to the west? The law of primogeniture, by which the oldest son inherits everything, was abolished in Canada in 1852,[1] and young Cornelius knew that his father would divide his land into parcels to be inherited by each of his sons; he further understood that a small plot would not produce enough sustenance for a potential family. Purchasing land on his own in Ontario might have been extremely difficult, because as a farm labourer, Cornelius would not have been able to earn or save enough money to make the purchase. Even if he did manage to buy some land, he would still have to build a house and buy farm implements and a horse for ploughing, riding, and driving—expenses he knew he could not afford. These factors might very well have been the main reasons for his departure from Upper Canada.

Cornelius may have intended to try his hand at other types of work out west in order to make enough money to purchase a small acreage back home in Upper Canada. The news of the gold strike on the Fraser River in 1858 would also have been enticing, as it was to other young men of his day—an entirely new venture that carried the possibility of untold wealth. He had big plans and needed to move away to fulfill them. Taking his chances in the West clearly appealed not only to his sense of adventure, but also to his desire for "more"—more land, more wealth, and more than a subsistent life. Land equalled wealth back then, just as it does now—young Cornelius would have known this. When he heard that good, arable land was being offered for next to nothing in British Columbia to those who possessed the wherewithal to work it, he decided to make his way there.

Although the O'Keefes had several children still at home when Cornelius chose to head west, the family must have had some misgivings about his decision; on the one hand, there would be one mouth fewer to feed, but on the other, there would also be one farmhand fewer to work the land. Added to this was the idea that Cornelius was about to head for a part of the country that none of them knew, during a time when travel was difficult at best. They knew that the chances of regular visits from their son were slim,

Go West, Young Man, Go West!

and communication by mail was unreliable. What would become of their son, travelling alone and with little money? Then again, Cornelius was not the first young man to abandon his home in Ontario to seek his fortune elsewhere. Their son was more than capable of doing the hard work necessary to provide for himself; perhaps this thought somewhat allayed their fears.

* * *

Cornelius took the only route west available: "to New York and from there by boat to the Isthmus of Panama and across the Isthmus... and then by boat, a Side Wheeler, up to San Francisco."[2] Once he arrived in the Cariboo area, he tried mining, unsuccessfully, and then he worked on the Cariboo Wagon Road.[3] By 1866, thanks to various endeavours, he had saved the considerable sum of $3,000.[4]

The necessity of a road that was navigable by wagons heading north was obvious to anyone who dared to travel the treacherous and extremely steep trails of the Cariboo Mountains. These were "hazardous trails over a rough country, crossing dizzy heights, crawling along the face of appalling precipices, [which] proved totally inadequate and the urgency for their betterment was at once recognized."[5] Travellers also encountered avalanches, deep snow, and river rapids, as well as illness, pests, and wild animals.[6] Even one of these obstacles would have deterred most men. Governor James Douglas himself recognized the urgent need for newer, more passable trails to the goldfields. He knew that "nothing short of a wagon road would meet the requirements [because] pack trains could make better time on a road than over dangerous trails."[7]

Terrain such as this would have made even the hardiest of men think twice about becoming part of the road-building crew. However, Cornelius's knowledge of clearing land for farming was useful in the building of the wagon road, and he worked on the Cariboo Wagon Road, perhaps until its completion "as far as Lillooet";[8] on November 10, 1862, he filed a pre-emption for land along the wagon road, across from a sixty-five-hectare parcel taken up by a William Robertson. He never occupied this land, though, so he apparently lost the claim.[9]

* * *

Once the road was passable, many people travelled it for reasons other than to make their fortunes in the goldfields. One of these travellers was Francis Jones Barnard, who later founded the BX Ranch near Vernon. Like O'Keefe, Barnard was an entrepreneur. He had "five dollars in his pockets as the sum total of his worldly wealth" and "began a career that always trended upward," beginning with securing "the mail contract to the Cariboo" in 1862.[10] However, his enterprise actually began in 1860, as he carried "letters and papers on his back,... travelling on foot from Yale to Cariboo, a [round-trip] distance of seven hundred and sixty miles"; postage was $2 per letter and $1 per newspaper.[11] Barnard made this 1,223-kilometre trip more than once during the 1862 season, although by this time he had purchased a horse that carried the burden while Barnard walked and led the way. As with many pioneers of his time, Barnard was an extremely enterprising man who was not afraid of hard work or adverse working conditions. The completion of the road meant that he could initiate the use of "four-horse stages with expert drivers."[12]

Go West, Young Man, Go West!

Many men tried to work on road-building crews, but often the road-building companies had "trouble getting white labor from the outset" and "experienced much difficulty obtaining payments from the government."[13] After being paid, many workers would simply quit their jobs and try their luck in the Cariboo goldfields, and if they became "disappointed fortune hunters, without money or food, driven to desperation, [they] resorted to robbery to obtain the means for satisfying their hunger, and sometimes murder [to fellow travellers] was done."[14] However, Barnard was never robbed, due to his "courage, vigilance, unwonted pluck, perseverance, and energy."[15] One of his other jobs in the West was supplying cordwood—which he transported on his back—to the town of Yale; he also became the town's constable, was the "purser on the steamer Yale" that plied the Fraser River, and was one of the road builders on "the trail up the Fraser River to Boston bar."[16]

Barnard and O'Keefe had this tendency to work toward ever-increasing prosperity in common. Barnard parlayed his mail contract into one of the longest-running stagecoach lines in North America; operating from 1861 until 1921, it was second only to Wells Fargo, which ran from 1852 until 1915, in the United States. By 1866, Barnard had "sole control of the express business from Yale to Barkerville."[17] In addition, in 1864, Barnard purchased 2,550 hectares of Crown land near Vernon where he raised and trained horses for use in his stage line enterprise. Perhaps he and O'Keefe crossed paths in the Cariboo region on one of Barnard's mail runs, and perhaps he mentioned to O'Keefe that there was good land available in the area where he himself had bought land. Barnard's express business was initially named Barnard's Express and Stage Line, incorporated in 1871 as "the British Columbia

Express Company."[18] The latter name was simply abbreviated to "the BX," and the area where Barnard's ranch was located is still called the BX.[19]

* * *

With his hopes of gold mining dashed, O'Keefe sought other ways to make money, and he decided to purchase cattle that he would then sell to successful gold miners. He was on his way to purchase some in 1866 when he met the British Thomas Wood on the trail near Little Shuswap Lake. Together, they herded Wood's cattle to the Big Bend on the Columbia River, north of present-day Revelstoke, BC. They soon travelled back to Oregon to purchase another herd of cattle, and there they met Thomas Greenhow of Newfoundland. The three men drove the cattle north, intending to sell them to the hungry gold miners. When the trio reached the north end of Okanagan Lake in June 1867, they saw the abundance of bunchgrass-covered grazing land, and realizing that the area would be prime cattle country, they decided to settle there. Their three-way partnership lasted until 1871, when Wood moved south to Winfield, now called Lake Country, after selling his land to Greenhow. He settled "at the foot of what was then called Long Lake" (now Kalamalka Lake). An opening was cut out of the south end of the lake to join it to Wood Lake. For a time, people called it "Woods Lake," perhaps because they thought of it as "Tom Woods Lake," since "he at one time owned most of the land around it," but now it is known simply as Wood Lake.[20]

O'Keefe and Greenhow were never partners in land purchases; each acquired land in his own right. Greenhow and Luc Girouard, considered to be Vernon's earliest pioneer, acquired a piece of

Go West, Young Man, Go West!

property by way of an 1884 Crown grant.[21] However, O'Keefe and Greenhow remained partners in cattle ventures until Greenhow's death in 1889, at which time his widow, Elizabeth, assumed control of her husband's holdings and became O'Keefe's partner in cattle ventures. Because O'Keefe believed, like most of his contemporaries, that having control of land would be the basis of his future wealth, he began acquiring land almost immediately.

CHAPTER

4

Birth of a Ranching Empire

O'KEEFE'S RANCHING EMPIRE began in June 1867, when he staked out that first pre-emption (land claim) of sixty-five hectares;[1] the claim was registered at Yale on July 25, 1868. On the Crown grant, O'Keefe's claim is listed below Greenhow's. It appears that together they thought out a plan for land acquisitions, one that included land with riparian water, which the men would purchase individually in the future.

O'Keefe continued for many years to buy or to assume control of large tracts of land in the North Okanagan and Spallumcheen areas. Crown grants were issued only after the pre-emptor could show proof of improvement, such as the clearing of land and planting of crops, or the construction of a permanent building; this often took several years to accomplish. The Crown grant for the 1867 claim, at the north end of Okanagan Lake, was issued

Birth of a Ranching Empire

on October 14, 1872.[2] O'Keefe erected a cabin in which to live; a small building on the property, currently in use as a chicken coop, is believed to have once been O'Keefe's cabin.[3] Deep Creek ran through O'Keefe's and Greenhow's property, providing the water so crucial for raising cattle.[4] O'Keefe's idea to earn enough money to purchase land back in Upper Canada changed in 1867 once he saw the luscious bunchgrass and realized that this land could sustain large numbers of cattle, so he changed his mind about moving home. This land in British Columbia was now his home.

Being one of the first to take up land in the area, O'Keefe was free to choose only land that he believed had the most potential in terms of water, pasturage, and winter grazing. Additionally, because he had been involved in the back-breaking work of clearing land on his family's concession in Upper Canada, he looked for land that was naturally clear, thereby allowing him to begin grazing cattle immediately, without the necessity of first removing trees. Lots and sections of land that he would purchase in the future were described as "1st class meadow land," "open grassy foot hills" having "good soil," "1st class farming land," and one with the "foot of [the] slope well drained."[5]

At that time, there were so few other ranchers with whom to compete for land that there was little need for O'Keefe to acquire larger tracts, and in addition, pre-emption laws forbade multiple claims. Because land was priced at the princely sum of one dollar per acre (or per 0.4 hectares), most ranchers could not afford to purchase property to which they already had free access.[6] Any revenue derived from this free land was pure profit, so that raising cattle, no matter how inferior their quality, would earn money for the rancher. Stock raisers allowed their cattle to mingle freely with those of their neighbours, and no one felt any need to improve breeds because everyone had more or less the same quality of animals. Buying a purebred bull was no guarantee that a particular owner's cows would be bred by the new bull, since all the animals shared the same grazing range. At the annual roundups, young calves went with their mothers to the cows' owners, while any stray calves were distributed among the participating cattlemen according to the size of their herds. Although the cattle market began to decline after the gold rush, O'Keefe increased his herd between 1868 and 1871, until he had to acquire more land to support the growing number of animals.

O'Keefe realized that he needed access to winter grazing pastures with sufficient quantities of the nutritious bunchgrass. This vegetation retains its nutritional value after the growing season and throughout the winter, so that during winters with light snowfall, cattle simply scrape off the snow to uncover their feed. However, O'Keefe knew that "overgrazing and the resultant destruction of winter grazing [would lead to] light cattle and large winter losses."[7] In other words, overgrazing meant that the grass would be eaten down to the roots to the degree that it would not be able to regrow and provide winter grazing.

The Land Ordinance of 1870 was the legislation that set the parameters for the use and purchase of Crown lands. It stated that

> pre-emptors were given four years after their claims had been surveyed within which to make payment... Only one pre-emption claim could be held at any one time, and the residence requirement called for continuous bona fide personal occupation [of] four-years duration.[8]

Birth of a Ranching Empire

The 1870 ordinance also allowed a pre-emptor to pay for his land in "four equal annual installments, [with] the first installment to be paid to the Commissioner at his office within three calendar months" of filing the claim.[9] Pre-emptions were the way the government ensured that people would settle on the land; they could then purchase it outright in installments, for which they would be given legal title, or Crown grant. On October 28, 1871, O'Keefe pre-empted for purchase another 194 hectares adjoining his first tract of land and paid a first installment of $240 the same month.[10] The Crown grant was provided on August 1, 1888.[11] This purchase gave O'Keefe 259 hectares on which to raise his cattle, but with his herd increasing naturally each year, he knew he would need even more land to sustain larger numbers of animals, which would then be driven to nearby markets. Over the next few years, he continued buying land that was beneficial to his ranching operation.

This same 1870 ordinance allowed a person living northeast of the Cascade Mountains to pre-empt a maximum of 129 hectares of unreserved Crown land. In April 1873, O'Keefe pre-empted another 129 hectares adjacent to the 1871 purchase near Okanagan Lake.[12] In 1874, he purchased 105 hectares from Greenhow, for which he paid $581.[13] Although the usual rate for land was still one dollar per acre, O'Keefe paid more than twice that amount for this particular piece of land because it was near Okanagan Lake and it presumably would be excellent winter grazing land. It also adjoined another acreage that O'Keefe wanted and would later buy.

In 1879, O'Keefe paid $320 for the east half of Section 3, Township 7, at the north end of Swan Lake; this acreage is likely the same piece of land that he pre-empted in 1873, even though the original certificate describes simply acreage on Okanagan Lake and includes no legal description.[14] O'Keefe now owned 388 hectares, for which he was taxed $40.[15] The discrepancy between the number of acres for which he was taxed (388 hectares) and the total number of acres that he claimed as his (517 hectares) is likely because the 320 acres (129 hectares) under dispute were not yet proven to be his legally. He was taxed only on the land to which he had legal title.

His real property in 1876 was assessed at $4,000, and his personal property at $8,000.[16] This personal wealth included his home and his general store, which he opened prior to his appointment as postmaster in 1872, and a flour mill that commenced operations in or before 1876. Grist mills were already operating elsewhere in the Okanagan, as "historic photos from Keremeos, Coldstream Ranch and O'Keefe Ranch" indicate.[17] Although the O'Keefe mill was similar to the other mills of the 1870s, it had been built after them, so it had a much-improved system using a turbine installed beneath the floor of the building. All the driving machinery was protected from the weather; an additional benefit was that O'Keefe could grind flour in the winter when the other mills were frozen.[18] A further advantage of the turbine was that it could operate efficiently with a low head of water, making possible the use of the quiet waters of Deep Creek as it flowed through the farmyard meadow.

* * *

While his herd continued to grow and bring him prosperity, O'Keefe earned even greater acceptance socially through his appointment as postmaster. The general store on his property was a central location to which mail was delivered for local residents. The distinction

Birth of a Ranching Empire

of having the "first Post Office in the Valley," which opened on August 14, 1872, and closed forty years later, on January 31, 1912, certainly increased his prestige among the local people.[19] His desire for respect is illustrated in a story told by Robert S. Hall, whose job entailed picking up the outgoing mail at O'Keefe's post office:

> One morning I had occasion to leave Vernon very early on the trip north, in order to catch the boat at Enderby, and was worrying because I had neglected to notify Mr. O'Keefe... I expected to have to pull him out of bed to get the mail ready for me, but when I rattled down the hill and drew up in front of his house... at the unearthly hour of four o'clock, there stood Connie O'Keefe at the door picking his teeth. "You are a little early this morning, aren't you?" was his only comment.[20]

"Connie," as he was known locally, wanted to ensure that, as postmaster, he earned the respect due his position, so he made certain not to miss Hall despite Hall's early arrival; he thought being late in meeting Hall might have diminished his respectability. In fact, O'Keefe's status probably increased in Hall's eyes as a result of the postmaster's obvious readiness even at that very early hour—or perhaps he was engaging in a game of "one-upmanship" with young Hall.

* * *

Although O'Keefe was becoming something of a land baron, even in these early years of his operation he needed someone to keep house for him, so sometime in the late 1860s or early 1870s, he invited a young woman from the Okanagan Nation named Rosie (or perhaps Rosa) to live with him (her Indigenous name was Alapetsa, but the fact that she also had a Christian name suggests that she had been baptized). Perhaps he lived with her in his original cabin. According to George J. Fraser, who worked for O'Keefe in the 1890s, O'Keefe "had an Indian woman for housekeeper during the early years of his ranch life" to whom he "had never been legally married."[21] These "country wives" were fairly common; as we will see, at least one other notable figure in the area also had an Indigenous wife. While no formal marriage appears in either civil or church records, the relationship O'Keefe had with Rosie was more than just a working one. They had at least two children, a boy and a girl. Rosie may even have refused to formalize the relationship, believing that O'Keefe would eventually end things with her when he decided to marry a white woman. In fact Fraser, O'Keefe's employee, noted that "she was apparently quite agreeable to accepting a gift of a few hundred dollars and returning to her native domicile" when that time came.

After leaving O'Keefe, Rosie and her daughter (two sons had drowned early in life) remained in the area. The 1881 census for the District of Yale, Sub-District of Priest's Valley, lists an Indigenous woman named Rosa, aged thirty-five, and a six-year-old girl named Christina; no father is identified. Ten years later, the census for the same area shows a seventeen-year-old Christine and a forty-year-old Rosie. While there is a discrepancy between the two records regarding Rosie's age (and Rosa's and Christine's names), Christine's age could very well be correct on both, depending on the date the information was taken. Also included as part of that family is a twenty-year-old Indigenous man named Isaac, who is probably the Isaac Harris who married Christine, "daughter of

Birth of a Ranching Empire

O'Keefe et Rosie" on May 15, 1891. The bride's age is shown as seventeen, indicating that she was born in 1874.[22] A marriage certificate testifies that "Isaac Harris, age 22 years, son of Harris, Englishman, and Mary, Native woman of Lillouet [sic], and Christine O'Keefe, age 17 years, daughter of O'Keefe and Rosie, Native woman" were, indeed, married on May 15, 1891.[23] Further evidence of Christine's paternity is found in the 1900 baptismal record of her daughter, which lists the child, Eva Harris, as the daughter of Isaac Harris and Christine O'Keefe. It has been suggested that the first knowledge Mary Ann O'Keefe (O'Keefe's first white wife) had of her husband's Indigenous family came when a young Indigenous boy went into the family's general store and tried to leave without paying for what he had chosen. When confronted by Mary Ann, he is reported to have told her to charge it to his father, "Conn O'Keefe."[24] While the source of this story might not be reliable, other evidence clearly indicates that O'Keefe had an Indigenous family, though he may not have chosen to acknowledge it.

What became of Rosie and her children is unclear, but it is likely that she remarried. The 1891 census for the District of Yale, Sub-District of Priest's Valley, shows that a man named Michele, aged forty-eight, had a forty-year-old wife named Rosie and an eight-year-old son named Alex. Also listed were a seventeen-year-old girl called Christine and a twenty-year-old man named Isaac, but their relationships to the family are recorded as unknown. No surnames are given for these people, but the first names suggest that they were O'Keefe's Indigenous companion, his daughter and her husband. Rosie likely had returned to her family, married and bore a son, Alex. Although the evidence is circumstantial, it is clear that O'Keefe had, at the very least, a common-law wife and a family prior to his marriage to Mary Ann. That Rosie was able to marry Michele is further evidence that she had never formalized her relationship with O'Keefe.

While having a common-law relationship with an Indigenous woman was not uncommon in the early years of settlement in British Columbia's interior, the practice was not completely accepted in all social circles. Another well-known and respected pioneer, E.J. Tronson, was married to an Indigenous woman named Nancy. In 1868, Tronson "pre-empted land on the eastern side of Okanagan Lake... and in 1885, with his partner, Charles Brewer, laid out the townsite of Centreville. He built and ran the old Victoria Hotel, and also operated a saw-mill at an early date."[25] Like O'Keefe, Tronson believed in education and was a trustee of the first school in Vernon, which opened in 1884, and which his three children attended.[26] Jean Barman writes that Tronson

> became a very respectable businessman in the budding community of Vernon. He had at least six children by his Native wife Nancy. C.W. Holliday, a young Englishman arriving there in 1889, did not know what to make of Tronson, perceiving him to be a "courtly-groomed gentleman. But to see him in church looking rather like a saintly old patriarch you would never have suspected... that on his ranch he maintained an Indian wife and a large half-breed family; a quite separate establishment, none of them ever appeared in public with him.[27]

Despite the perceived "handicap" of an Indigenous wife, Tronson was highly regarded by most people. Today, there is a road along the shore and on the hill above Okanagan Lake named in his honour.

CHAPTER

5

The Rancher Finds a Wife

ALTHOUGH OTHER MEN maintained long-term relationships with Indigenous women, as a Catholic, O'Keefe may have believed that a true marriage must be sanctified by the Church, and that an unsanctified arrangement, such as the one he had with Rosie, would be deemed unacceptable not only by the Church, but also by society in general. Perhaps he felt that a relationship with an Indigenous woman would hinder his plans to become a respected member of the area's future society. In 1876, he travelled back to Fallowfield, where he married Mary Ann McKenna, and in doing so, married above his own family's social position.

There is no clear evidence that Cornelius O'Keefe had known his bride for very long, but one can surmise at least that he was aware of her family. In Upper Canada during the 1870s, neighbours several kilometres apart would have socialized occasionally.

Given that the O'Keefes lived in the same general area as the McKennas, it seems fairly certain that the two families would have known each other, particularly since they probably attended the same church. Cornelius would probably have known that Mary Ann was still unmarried, and because he was not exactly a stranger to her family, he may have chosen to court her formally. A ten-year age difference was not uncommon during this time, as a young man would need to be able to support a wife, and it would take him some time to become sufficiently self-supporting in his career. Again, since there is no proof that they were romantically involved prior to his move west, one has to imagine that perhaps he had begun a written correspondence with her before going east in 1876, preparing the way for their marriage, which was recorded at Fallowfield on November 20, 1877, in St. Patrick's Church.[1]

Both he and Mary Ann had their photographs taken in Montreal in 1876. The photographer's numbers on the backs of the pictures indicate that the photos were taken at the same time, so it is reasonable to conclude that they were engagement pictures. In the photo, in which O'Keefe is almost forty years of age, his hairline is receding, although the colour is still dark. Mary Ann, nearly thirty years old, has her hair drawn back severely from her face. Her rather elaborate jewellery suggests that either her family was wealthy enough to be able to afford to buy such things, or that O'Keefe had the funds to buy them for her. She looks contemplative, and it is tempting to consider what she might have been thinking. Would she ever see her family again? Would she be happy in her new life? What would she encounter on the trip west, or in her new home? How many other women were in the area, and would she meet them and form friendships with them?

The Rancher Finds a Wife

Cornelius and Mary Ann McKenna O'Keefe, 1876.
COURTESY OF THE HISTORIC O'KEEFE RANCH

All of these thoughts surely occurred to her, and like any woman of her time who faced such a daunting journey, she would have had some misgivings regardless of the method of travel. Her husband would have given her some idea of the house he had built for her, but he had no pictures to show her; he had only words to express the scope of the building and its conveniences. Nevertheless, her pioneering spirit obviously prevailed, and they set off for what must have seemed like a life in the wilderness, away from family, friends, and anything familiar.

* * *

The railway connecting central Canada to the west coast was still a decade in the future, so the O'Keefes' journey west promised to be long and difficult—not all that different from his first journey west. They could travel over land, by horse and wagon, by water, or by rail via a circuitous route through the United States. Any possible overland route was fraught with many dangers: wild animals; extreme weather conditions throughout the fall, winter, and spring; and treacherous and potentially impassable paths used mostly by traders and Indigenous peoples. If roads existed, they were not paved, of course, so the route would have been, at best, dirt or gravel, both of which would turn to a morass of mud during and after any precipitation. There really were no easily navigable east–west land routes; the sea route was very long and entailed going around Cape Horn at the southern tip of South America—a trip of several months.

The third and most efficient option, and the one they chose, was by rail via the United States: first a train to New York, and then west to San Francisco. The Union Pacific had been running east–west trips for several years; the earliest passenger service commenced in May 1869, with the New York to San Francisco trip taking under a week. While this was certainly the preferred method of travel, it was not without its own inconveniences. In the seven or eight years of its existence, the Union Pacific made some improvements to its passenger trains, but they were still "undeniably crude; they seldom travelled more than [twenty] miles per hour and meals were eaten quickly in station dining halls. Wooden benches were the standard seating accommodations and wood stoves furnished heat."[2]

Once they reached San Francisco, O'Keefe and his new bride took a steamer up to Victoria, British Columbia, and then another boat to Vancouver. Although O'Keefe undoubtedly had the financial means to pay for a comfortable cabin, the trip north had the complications of rough weather, poor food, and often seasickness.

The Rancher Finds a Wife

From Vancouver, they travelled by stagecoach or by horseback to the Interior; they likely boarded a BC Express (formerly BX Express) stagecoach at Soda Creek, about 250 kilometres from Ashcroft, for the remainder of the trip; in fact, since O'Keefe's ranch was the terminus, he and Mary Ann would have disembarked and been home immediately. She must have felt a strong sense of accomplishment at having arrived safely.

* * *

For its time, the house Mary Ann found waiting for her was quite modern, with a wood-burning stove in the kitchen, a dining room, and two separate bedrooms on the second floor. It also boasted a parlour with north- and east-facing windows, allowing for the most light, on the main floor. The walls were even papered. Because wallpaper would not adhere to the rough logs, they were whipsawn to flatten them somewhat. Cheesecloth was then stretched and tacked onto the logs. This material would have been wet or at least damp when it was stretched; as it dried, it would shrink, leaving a much smoother surface onto which the wallpaper was glued. The effect was that the paper looked quite flat against the walls, belying the unevenness of the round logs. Perhaps O'Keefe had added this touch to the walls to make the house more appealing to his new bride.

Mary Ann would have wasted little time in turning the house into a home for herself, her husband, and their future family. The first of nine children was born in 1879, two years after the wedding.

CHAPTER

6

Land Disputes

WHILE O'KEEFE MAY have gained social standing through his marriage, he continued earning respectability through land ownership. He sought to increase his landholdings by whatever means he could—including manipulating the law to get what he wanted occasionally. While he was in Ontario for his wedding, a dispute arose over the 129-hectare parcel of land that he had pre-empted in 1873. This pre-emption contravened the 1870 land ordinance on at least two major points: occupation and improvements to the claim, as well as absence from the claim.

While it might seem that he contravened the Act regarding multiple claims, this was not technically the case. The 1870 Act stated that no one was allowed to hold more than one claim through pre-emption; people who tried to pre-empt a second claim would "forfeit all right, title, and interest to the prior claim recorded by

Land Disputes

him."[1] However, because O'Keefe had already received a Crown grant certificate for his first pre-emption of 65 hectares and had begun paying for his 194-hectare parcel, he was not in contravention of this particular section of the Act. It seems that the main argument against O'Keefe's second pre-emption of 129 hectares of surveyed land was that he had not yet received a Crown grant for the 1871 pre-emption of those 194 previous hectares.

In September of 1877, when O'Keefe was no doubt preparing for his November wedding, the commissioner of lands and works, C.A. Vernon, wrote to Indian Reserve Commissioner Gilbert Sproat to convey his concerns about O'Keefe's use of the land he had pre-empted in 1873. The Okanagan Nation people believed that this land should be part of their reserve. Vernon wrote to Sproat because Sproat was working on a commission to investigate the problem of finding sufficient reserve land for Indigenous people: "It was difficult to extend the Indians' inadequate reserve [at the head of Okanagan Lake] because all the land of any value had been taken up by settlers" such as O'Keefe.[2] Vernon could not ascertain whether or not O'Keefe had "complied with the requirements of the Land Act under which he [had] pre-empted" that land, because he had not been commissioner at the time O'Keefe pre-empted it.[3] Vernon believed O'Keefe had never actually occupied the land in question.[4] The Act clearly stated that any pre-emptor must prove to the land commissioner, in writing and with two other people as witnesses, that he had lived on the pre-empted claim and had improved the land with crops or permanent buildings to a value of at least $2.50 per acre (0.4 hectares).[5] It is not surprising that when Sproat wrote to Greenhow asking him to verify O'Keefe's occupancy, Greenhow "decline[d] to answer";[6]

47

O'Keefe had not appointed anyone to speak on his behalf regarding land matters while he was away, so his partner Greenhow was powerless to deal with the issue.

O'Keefe probably knew his claim might not have been strictly legal, but he believed that the occupation requirement did not apply to his 129-hectare claim.[7] O'Keefe's absence was itself part of the problem, though. In late September 1877, Father I.M. Baudre, a Catholic missionary from the Okanagan Mission who had first corresponded with the commissioner of lands and works on behalf of the Okanagan Nation, then wrote to Sproat at the behest of two Indigenous people, Bazile and Aleck, who said that O'Keefe had never resided on the property.[8] The ordinance stated that a pre-emptor had the right "to be absent from his claim for any one period not exceeding two months during any one year [and]... shall be deemed to have permanently ceased to occupy his claim when he shall have been absent, continuously, for a longer period than two months."[9] O'Keefe was certainly gone from 1876 through to 1877, far more than the two-month time limit, so he was clearly in contravention of the Act. Sproat therefore wrote to O'Keefe and informed him that his claim had been cancelled. Sproat also wrote to Vernon and said that because O'Keefe had defaulted on his claim by not fulfilling the obligations of pre-emption, he forfeited to the Crown any buildings and improvements he had made. Sproat further recommended that O'Keefe have until March 1, 1878, to remove his property. However, this ruling did not end the dispute.

O'Keefe's lawyers, Drake and Jackson, were of the opinion that it was not the commissioners' job to apply for the cancellation of records, but Sproat said they were wrong.[10] The ordinance

Land Disputes

stated that the commissioner had the right to "cancel the claim of the pre-emptor" once the official was sure of the claimant's cessation of occupation, so it was within Sproat's jurisdiction to cancel O'Keefe's pre-emption because he had not occupied it. Sproat went on to say that the commissioners "in reality" meant that O'Keefe's claim was "cancelled by his own default."[11] Sproat said that O'Keefe simply recorded the land in question and only did

> a little ploughing and fencing on it, and by this he seems to have considered that he acquired a title to the land under the 1870 Act... The homestead must be on the pre-emption and the man must continuously live there; this is what the law says... Mr. O'Keefe is not a poor ignorant settler, but a wealthy intelligent cattle farmer, already in possession of 640 acres near the piece of land in question. It is right to expect that he should strictly conform to the plain meaning of the law.[12]

It is obvious that Sproat had little use for O'Keefe's tactics in handling the situation, and subsequent letters to Vernon illustrate Sproat's desire to settle the problem. He noted that the Indigenous people were questioning "the Queen's authority to dispose of their lands without having extinguished their title to the soil." Sproat said that he believed that the commissioner's authority was being weakened "by the delay in adjusting the question with Mr. O'Keefe."[13] The dispute continued, with the Indigenous people appealing to officials for a resolution.

Philip Girod, a neighbour in Spallumcheen, wrote to the Indian Reserve commissioner on behalf of the local Indigenous people to say that they had informed O'Keefe of the commissioner's decision to give the land to them. In April of 1879, O'Keefe replied that the commissioner "had no right to give his land away," and said he would give it up only if he were "paid for it."[14] Not only did O'Keefe believe that he owned the land, but he was willing to circumvent the law to get what he wanted, unless he was also compensated. O'Keefe was acting under the advice of his lawyers, Drake and Jackson, who had written to the attorney general that they had "advised Mr. O'Keefe to resist all attempts of the Indians to interfere with his land, crops, or property, by force if necessary."[15]

Sproat wrote to the superintendent of Indian Affairs in Ottawa that he no longer knew what to tell the Indigenous people when they asked what was being done to end the dispute. He said that "in continuing to assure [the] Okanagan Indians that the matter… [was] receiving effective attention, [he was] stating what [was] probably not quite true."[16] Chief Chilliheetsa of the Upper Nicola Band near Kamloops wrote to Sproat in October of 1879 and said that the Okanagan people were prepared to take possession of the land by force. He informed Sproat that O'Keefe had "built a mill on the creek in which the Indians fish" and had "diverted the water" and "threaten[ed] the Indians when they remonstrated with him."[17] He said his advice to the Okanagans was to wait for Sproat's answer before taking any action.

Sproat's final letter regarding this matter appears to have been the one written on July 17, 1878, to the chief commissioner of lands and works. In it, Sproat asked the commissioner whether he had cancelled O'Keefe's claim, and if he had not, what he planned to do about the matter. O'Keefe's lawyers also wrote to the chief commissioner of lands and works in August of 1878 and asked that

Land Disputes

he investigate the entire affair so that "some arrangement" could be made.[18] Apparently, the provincial government did nothing to ameliorate the problem. While the commissioner "decided to give some of the land claimed by the settlers to the Indians," this decision "was not ratified by the provincial government."[19] Whether Sproat continued his correspondence with the Okanagan people is unclear; suffice to say that he was at a loss to explain to them why the land was not returned to them.

The entire matter appears to have been swept under the table; O'Keefe retained possession of the land for at least a few years. This affair was not unusual, nor was the apparent lack of fairness. Reserves for Indigenous people had to "conform to every letter of the law," in order to "meet with the approval of the provincial government," according to historian Robin Fisher. At the same time "all kinds of laxity was permitted with settlers' pre-emptions."[20] It appears that this "laxity" was applied in this case. O'Keefe used procrastination, evasion of the law, and outright threats to keep the land to which he claimed ownership. There is some speculation that, after a long delay, someone quietly paid O'Keefe for the land in dispute.

CHAPTER

7

More Wealth, More Prestige

O'KEEFE APPEARS TO have won the battle over the disputed land (at least for a while), and he continued to acquire land and stock animals. By 1879, he and Greenhow had amassed eight hundred cattle, ten hogs, and eighty-five horses. They each owned 391 hectares of land. Compared to other pioneering ranchers in the area—Price Ellison, Augustus Schubert, and A.L. Fortune—these numbers were quite impressive. These three men each possessed 129 hectares of land. Ellison had only two horses, Schubert had six, and Fortune thirteen. The only rancher who surpassed O'Keefe and Greenhow was F.G. Vernon, who had one thousand head of cattle, twelve hogs, seventy-five horses, and 1,242 hectares of land.[1] Charles Frederick Houghton, the founder of the Coldstream Ranch, had six hundred head of cattle, six horses, seventy-five hogs,

More Wealth, More Prestige

and 391 hectares. Even in those early years of the industry, O'Keefe was among the foremost ranchers in the area. However, while O'Keefe owned a great deal of land, he also continued to pasture animals in the common rangelands, competing with the growing number of settlers who had access to those same rangelands. With "all unreserved surveyed land in the Osoyoos District... thrown open to pre-emption and purchase,... the threat of losing access to it prompted... the decision to purchase" more land over which he would have sole control.[2] Obtaining exclusive ownership of large acreages meant that O'Keefe could avoid having to share the precious bunchgrass and water with other ranchers. Any riparian water found on that land was his, and such ownership also gave him the right to erect fences that would exclude all but his own animals. O'Keefe took the competition for access to key land seriously, and on July 30, 1883, he bought four lots comprising 289 hectares in Okanagan Landing from Charles Frederick Houghton, for a total of $7,000, or approximately $9.79 per acre (0.4 hectares).[3]

* * *

As a member of the British military, Houghton was entitled to a military claim of 587 hectares. He served during the Crimean War and participated in suppressing the 1885 Riel Resistance, and also "shared in the actions at Fish Creek and Batoche." He also very actively supported Canadian Confederation.[4] While the size of the land claim for military people was disputed by the colonial government, which wanted to reduce it to 121 hectares, Houghton eventually received the full 587 hectares. He opted for land in the vicinity of Okanagan Lake, calling his acreage the Coldstream Ranch.[5] Although he could certainly have taken land anywhere within the British dominion, he chose the Okanagan Valley; perhaps he hoped for agricultural progress similar to that envisioned by his contemporaries, including O'Keefe, Ellison and Fortune. The September 22, 1927, edition of the *Vernon News* reported that in 1864 Houghton had called the Okanagan Valley "The Fields of Ardath in the year 1864," a reference to the gardens of Babylon and the image of fruitfulness they evoke, similar to the lushness of the Okanagan Valley.[6]

Augustus Schubert, another early pioneer, was among the Overlanders of 1862 who travelled west from Red River.[7] He and his wife, Catherine, settled near what is now Enderby, and in 1884 settled west of Lansdowne, near Armstrong. The epitome of the true pioneer, she travelled with her three small children while pregnant with a fourth. Overlander leader Thomas McMicking wrote of Catherine Schubert that she had "accomplished a task to which but few women are equal" and "one which but few *men* would have the courage to undertake." The day after her arrival in Kamloops, Catherine gave birth to her daughter, Rose, who was delivered by several Secwepemc women, and who was so "named for the rosehips the family had eaten to stave off starvation."[8] Rose is generally believed to be the first Caucasian child born in the Interior of British Columbia. The Schuberts were, like O'Keefe and Ellison, strong believers in the value of education, and they sent their children to "the first official school in the North Okanagan... the Round Prairie School built on the farm of Augustus Schubert in 1885."[9]

* * *

More Wealth, More Prestige

Like most of his fellow pioneers, O'Keefe must have had a master plan for acquiring good land, and his real estate purchases were not random. Not only did every purchase increase his landholdings but every purchase was also either along a body of water or contiguous to land owned by his partners, Thomas and Elizabeth Greenhow. It was important to both O'Keefe and Greenhow to own land over which they would have exclusive use. Several of O'Keefe's purchases adjoined land that he already owned, while others had lake frontage. Another adjoined some of Greenhow's land, and yet another adjoined an acreage that O'Keefe would buy in 1892. The real value of purchasing land with these advantages was to become evident only after thirty years, as we shall see. O'Keefe had an almost uncanny ability to foresee agricultural trends and practices.

In January and February of 1884, O'Keefe published notices of his intention to purchase sixty-five hectares of land "commencing at the south-west corner of Section 20, Township 9," which was about midway between Okanagan Lake and Long Lake.[10] Two years later, another notice stated his intention to purchase the southeast quarter of Section 20, Township 9, which adjoined the 1884 purchase, and the northwest quarter of Section 21, Township 9.[11] He was building a ranch of the size that people took note of, and one it appears people may have taken exception to as well. Michael Hagan, who wrote about his travels through the Okanagan Valley, commented in 1884 "that the immense ranches... containing over 5,000 acres each" had "a great tendency to prevent necessary settlers" in the Okanagan Valley, although he allowed that it was "natural that man should increase his property and power."[12]

O'Keefe's capital for buying land came from his cattle sales, very often to J.B. Greaves, the manager of a syndicate that supplied beef to the Canadian Pacific Railway. During the 1880s, Greaves made regular cattle purchases from the ranchers in the Okanagan by making a "cash deposit" first and then arranging "favourable terms for the balance," or else he would "secure a very good bargain with an immediate cash payment in full." He acted as a bank for "many Okanagan ranchers who were badly cut off from a market," providing a way for them to "pay their taxes, wages, and other expenses." Greaves arrived in the Okanagan in February of 1882, and planned to purchase 3,000 to 3,500 head of cattle; clearly, there was no single stock raiser who could supply all of Greaves' cattle needs, so it is safe to assume that O'Keefe was one of those who supplied at least part of that demand. By mid-1885, Greaves and his partners "had spent $170,000 on close to 8,500 cattle from other Interior ranches." Greaves "was establishing the Interior cattle market by paying $35 a head for three-year-old steers and $30 a head for two-year-old steers and fat cows."[13] It is certain that O'Keefe saw some of that money, and despite the alleged displeasure of other area settlers, he continued to acquire land while at the same time increasing his standing as a shrewd cattleman.

* * *

O'Keefe's standing in the community was greatly enhanced in 1882 when he and his wife hosted the Marquis of Lorne, the governor general of Canada. The marquis stayed with the O'Keefes in their log home, and the visit was recorded in the November 9 edition of the *Inland Sentinel*, which stated that O'Keefe's home was "the favoured stopping place." The governor general's party "remained

More Wealth, More Prestige

at Mr. O'Keefe's from Saturday evening until Wednesday" to hunt game.[14] At the end of the visit, the Marquis of Lorne presented O'Keefe with

> a twelve gauge shot gun. This gun, manufactured by the Wesley Richards Company of London England, [had] a fine damascus barrel and elaborate scrollwork and, in keeping with its owner's reputation for fine things, [was] one of the finest money could buy at the time.[15]

Hosting such a guest was prestigious for anyone, but for an Irish Catholic, it would have been even more so. After all, the marquis was *royalty*, and a member of the Church of England to boot. To host such an important guest in their home must have made the O'Keefes immensely proud.

But space was tight in the O'Keefes' two-bedroom log home, which housed O'Keefe, his wife, and four children, including two toddlers. The marquis and his wife would have been given Mary Ann and Cornelius's bedroom for the duration of the visit, and the hosts would have shared their children's room. But did the O'Keefes complain about this inconvenience? Hardly! They were probably the envy of their neighbours both near and far. The governor general, along with his party and hosts, went hunting for the game birds that were so plentiful in the area, and perhaps Mary Ann cooked the fowl. In any case, "it was not bachelor cooking he got."[16] Mary Ann was very busy with her children and working in the store, as well as playing hostess to the governor general and his entourage. It is difficult to envision what the visit must have meant for her: cooking, cleaning, and caring for her children while

Vanguard of the Pine near Okanagan Lake, by the Marquis of Lorne, 1882. The O'Keefe home is just left of centre. The topography the governor general observed in 1882 is much the same today.
COURTESY OF THE ROYAL BC MUSEUM AND ARCHIVES, PDP02132

at the same time ensuring that the guests were taken care of and given every consideration. She likely heaved a sigh of relief when they left!

The marquis was clearly pleased with his hosts and his accommodations, because in addition to the fine gift of the shotgun, he made a sketch of the scenery he had observed during his hunting excursions and presented it to the O'Keefes upon his departure. This was another honour; few people could claim ownership of artwork done by a member of the British royalty. The marquis entitled his sketch *Vanguard of the Pine near Okanagan Lake*, and dated it October 11, 1882.

More Wealth, More Prestige

The marquis and his party visited other farms in the area, including those of other local pioneers, such as Moses Lumby and A.L. Fortune—only those ranches that were large and well established, with ranchers actively involved in the community.[17] Lumby and Fortune were appointed as justices of the peace in 1877.[18]

* * *

Lumby, after whom the village of Lumby is named, was an enterprising man involved in various types of work, including prospecting, farming, and ranching. The *Vernon News* reported in 1893 that Lumby spent one summer in the late 1860s

> in the Big Bend, where he had taken the contract of carrying the mails and express from Bonaparte into the Big Bend. His route here was 22 miles by foot, then a long distance by row boat up the Thompson and Shuswap lake to Seymour from which point he had to pack the mails and express on his back.[19]

In addition, he was instrumental in establishing the Shuswap and Okanagan Railway, and was its first vice president. He "was involved with the liquor licencing court, president of the Agricultural Society, President of the Enderby Athletic Club," and in 1892, "he chaired Vernon's incorporation meeting as well as hospital meetings. He was on the Ways and Means Committee of the Anglican Church construction project."[20] He became the government agent in Vernon in 1892.[21]

Like Lumby and O'Keefe, Fortune kept busy with various ventures, including farm work at Lillooet and mine work in the Big Bend mines; in 1866, he staked a land claim near Enderby, and on

June 18, 1867, he "obtained [a] crown grant for two claims of 348 acres (Lot 148)." He had a strong religious commitment as well, and aided the missionaries "by founding the first Sunday School in the northern part of the valley," and he "was also the first elder of the Presbyterian Church in the Valley."[22] Being a justice of the peace in a frontier community was a "position of leadership and responsibility. This speaks well for his integrity and leadership qualities."[23] Clearly, O'Keefe was keeping company with some well-respected people.

In addition to his other duties and commitments, O'Keefe was involved with the military. Having likely been involved in a militia unit in Ontario in the 1850s, O'Keefe continued his military affiliation in the Spallumcheen area in 1884. The "Spallumcheen and Okanagan" section of the *Inland Sentinel* noted that people in the area were organizing a "Mounted Rifle Company," and "a healthier, smarter and better lot of men [could] not be brought together in the Dominion." The writer noted that the men were "all accustomed to the saddle," "excellent horsemen, with the best of horses." Not only that, but because they were all "such property holders as Messrs. O'Keefe, Greenhow, etc.," the writer was sure of "a satisfactory result."[24] Such a company would be of tremendous help should any "disturbance take place during the building of the railway through the mountains or elsewhere along the line of our Public Works."[25] The military company was mentioned in the paper a few months later, when Michael Hagan travelled through the area. He saw a "large number of men" at O'Keefe's post office, and at first he thought "Captain O'Keefe had his Mountain Rifle Company in readiness," but then he learned that O'Keefe "was

More Wealth, More Prestige

intending to assemble his force as soon as his commission, which [was] soon expected, arrived."

As a captain and founding member of such an organization, O'Keefe would have commanded the respect not only of the men in his company, but of the general public as well. However, it seems that the captain's commission O'Keefe expected never materialized. Three years later, in 1887, O'Keefe was appointed provincial justice of the peace—a further affirmation of his political acceptance.[26]

CHAPTER

8

Additions, Achievements, and Accolades

BY 1885, O'KEEFE had planned a large addition to the log house in which he had lived since 1876 that would double the size of the original structure. He could also afford to buy beautiful clothes and jewellery for his wife. A photograph of Mary Ann from around 1885 shows her hair done in an attractive and stylish manner; she is no longer the plain, severe-looking woman of her engagement photograph some nine years earlier. Her dress has braiding and beadwork on the bodice, and she wears a beautiful brooch that appears in later photographs as well. She seems somewhat more confident and self-assured, too. And why should she not be? She was married to a successful rancher, lived in a lovely home, had several children, worked in her husband's general store, and managed the household.

Additions, Achievements, and Accolades

Mary Ann O'Keefe, ca. 1885.
COURTESY OF THE HISTORIC O'KEEFE RANCH

However, Mary Ann's life was not without tragedy. Both the O'Keefes and the Greenhows had sons born in late summer of 1883. On October 11, 1883, the *Inland Sentinel* reported the death, on September 23, of "the only son of Mr. Thomas Greenhow, aged about [two] months," and on the same day, of "the infant son of Mr. C. O'Keefe, aged about three weeks."[1] The cause was believed to be influenza. Both families grieved their loss immensely.

Despite being very busy, Mary Ann had made some friends, mostly the wives of other local pioneers, and generally lived a good life with a man who loved her. She had hosted royalty by this time, and she had learned how to present herself in a more flattering way. All the questions that had shown in her face in her engagement photo had been answered.

First addition to the log house, finished in 1886 (photo dates to 1887).
COURTESY OF THE VERNON MUSEUM AND ARCHIVES

* * *

The addition to the log house was completed in 1886, and it was later dubbed the "mansion." Hagan found the house to be "one of the finest in the country, and... furnished regardless of expense."[2] In a photograph of the house after its completion, O'Keefe stands in the left foreground, looking very proud of his latest accomplishment. The house had a bay window in the parlour and a veranda along the front and one side. Three stories high, the addition boasted seven rooms.

O'Keefe hired a cabinetmaker to do the woodwork, which included an elaborate staircase (still in fine shape) that was constructed using the blind mortise and tenon method.[3] The handrail is asymmetrical; the groove in one side is deeper than in the other so that it fits the hand perfectly and allows a firm grip whether

Additions, Achievements, and Accolades

ascending or descending. Other details in the house point to O'Keefe's willingness to spare no expense. From the ornate hand-carved corner-pieces of the door and window frames to the beautiful stained glass window at the foot of the stairs, to the large guest bedroom complete with five windows, the house was modern and elegant, no doubt the result of Mary Ann O'Keefe's good taste. The O'Keefe home was truly a showpiece in which nothing but the finest would suffice.

O'Keefe's involvement in the Catholic Church continued, and in the 1880s, he and his wife instituted a subscription to raise money for building a church. His family back in his home parish of Fallowfield, Ontario, would have witnessed, if not participated in, building the first church of any denomination in the area. The first written reference to this church is dated June 17, 1832, when the priest from Bytown, later Ottawa, recorded the baptism of four children in "the New Church of Nepean"; this was the church that "the Tipperary Irish" had raised in 1832, "a small log chapel called St Jude's on the Richmond Road."[4] Later, the nearby Tierney family, led by patriarch Denis Tierney, a successful farmer from Tipperary, Ireland, hosted Mass in his son James's "fine three-storey stone house," built in 1860.[5] This small church was later replaced by St. Patrick's Catholic Church in Fallowfield, which "was blessed on 21 October 1866."[6]

Perhaps O'Keefe wished to follow what he saw as a family tradition—to again be part of building the first Roman Catholic church in his adopted home, the Okanagan Valley. He donated the land for both the new church and the cemetery beside it, and he also made the largest contribution of $150; Elizabeth Greenhow donated $100, even though her husband was not Catholic.

Other subscribers included such well-known locals as Price Ellison and Eli Lequime. Many others pledged amounts of as much as fifty dollars and as little as fifty cents.[7] Perhaps because O'Keefe's birthday was July 26, the Feast of Saint Ann, he asked the Oblate priests to christen the church "St. Ann's." While this shows a certain amount of conceit on O'Keefe's part, it illustrates his need for approval from both the Church and his fellow parishioners, as well as the degree of his influence over the Oblates. It is doubtful that the priests would have—or even could have—refused his request, given that he was the major financial sponsor for the building, as well as the donor of the land upon which the church was built. The new church was blessed, and the first service was held on December 25, 1889.[8]

When Thomas Greenhow died in 1889, O'Keefe decreed that he be buried outside the cemetery fence because he was not Catholic. Later, he thought better of his decision, probably because Greenhow had been an exemplary business partner, and had the fence moved so that it enclosed Greenhow's grave.

Less than two years after the church's first service, the O'Keefes took up another subscription, this time to purchase an organ for the church. Again, O'Keefe donated the largest amount, with Elizabeth Greenhow, Eli Lequime, and E.J. Tronson contributing lesser amounts.[9] In addition to the status that came with having donated both land and money for the construction of the church and the purchase of the church organ, churchgoers would also pass by his general store, thereby potentially earning more sales. Having the church established on his property also meant that he occasionally hosted visiting clergy. In June 1891, Bishop Durien of New Westminster stayed with the O'Keefes. He "held a

Additions, Achievements, and Accolades

confirmation service" and music was played on the new organ.[10] Seven years later, the O'Keefes entertained the "Right Reverend Bishop Dontonville, D.D., O.M.I., of New Westminster."[11]

* * *

With his place in the church firmly established, O'Keefe continued to host parties in his home where he was reportedly unstinting in his generosity; these social events were often mentioned in the local newspaper. The December 29, 1892, edition of the *Vernon News* said that "the Christmas attendance was larger than usual and did ample justice to the feast provided." In 1897, the paper reported that "Mr. and Mrs. O'Keefe gave a delightful dance at their beautiful and spacious residence." While the number of guests "exceeded eighty, at no time were the spacious rooms overcrowded."[12] An O'Keefe employee said that O'Keefe "was very generous in some ways and very miserly in other ways," and that "he hung on to the nickels, but when he threw a party everyone was welcome and he had champagne—all [a person] could drink."[13]

Mary Ann O'Keefe pursued her own accomplishments, including earning local exhibition prizes for her bread, preserves, and needlework.[14] She and Elizabeth Greenhow shared the platform when the Countess of Aberdeen presided at the Women's National Council of Canada in 1895;[15] in August of 1898, Mary Ann and Lady Aberdeen attended a meeting where they discussed finding a nurse from the Victorian Order of Nurses for the hospital.[16] Lady Aberdeen mentioned the Women's Council in her journal, in which she discussed the work of the council at a local agricultural show, indicating that she believed that the council's work in "opening a Cottage Hospital" was important for the area. The work of the council "sought to improve the political, social, and economic position of women and... founded the Victorian Order of Nurses." At the agricultural show in Vernon in 1896, the local "Women's Council had the charge of all the industrial part and of the bread and butter and made quite a success of it."[17] Lady Aberdeen and Mary Ann were clearly well acquainted. The O'Keefes socialized with the Aberdeens and were "present at a ball given by Lord and Lady Aberdeen" in 1896.[18] Mary Ann O'Keefe was also a strong supporter of the Vernon Jubilee Hospital, to which she donated chickens and milk.[19]

CHAPTER

9

Cattle Baron to Land Baron

BY THE LATE 1880S, O'Keefe began to increase his wheat production. As a boy growing up in Ontario and later as a visitor to the east, he had seen first-hand the positive effects of having a railway nearby, so he knew that the soon-to-be-completed railway would provide the necessary transportation for large grain crops. It would give O'Keefe much easier access to larger markets. However, without more efficient farm machinery, the planting and harvesting of large crops was very difficult, but purchasing new equipment required money. He pre-sold his 1887 wheat crop. His expenditures added up quickly: the bill from the Columbia Milling Company for advance shipping charges on the steamer *Red Star* totalled $623.43,[1] and not surprisingly, just four days later, he ordered a Brantford binder at the cost of $280, as well as a J.O. Wisner seed drill with sixteen hoes for $145, both from

Nicholles and Renouf, a farm supply store in Victoria.[2] While the new machinery was expensive, the potential benefits of owning such modern equipment far outweighed the cost. By December of 1889, he had 113 hectares planted in fall wheat.[3]

In May 1891, the *Vernon News* reported that O'Keefe had brought into the "N.E. office a stalk of fall wheat standing 4'6" high, the ear of which is fully formed, an average sample from a field of 80 acres (32 hectares)." O'Keefe predicted that the year would "witness very heavy crops all through the district on account of the late rains." His methods and machinery were paying off, and less than two months later, O'Keefe had cut 121 hectares of fall wheat, had another 142 hectares of spring wheat yet to cut, and was using "two binders (an Osborne and his Brantford) to accomplish the task." In addition, he had twenty hectares of oats and forty hectares of wheat for hay to cut; the paper reported in August that "all his crops" were "splendid" and could "hardly be excelled throughout the district." In October, the paper said that O'Keefe thought he would "put up about five hundred tons of hay" and would "winter one thousand head of cattle."[4] Hagan reported in December of 1891 that O'Keefe's expectations had been met, since he had had "700 acres under grain" the previous season, with some cut for feed, and had "500 tons dispatched to the Columbia Flouring Mill, and he planned "to place more acreage under grain" next season.[5]

* * *

The completion in 1885 of the trans-national railway brought with it the possibility of increasing the marketability of O'Keefe's cattle. Not only could a railway deliver goods and equipment necessary to his business, but it could also take products produced on the ranch

Cattle Baron to Land Baron

to markets near or far. As a shrewd businessman, he realized that people would prefer to purchase top-quality products, just like he did, if they could get them, and he intended to have high-quality cattle for that new market. After all, why would one choose to buy products of inferior quality if better quality items were available? In the case of breeding stock, a higher-quality animal would produce better offspring, which in turn would fetch higher prices at market. He knew that the increased competition from the Alberta cattle industry necessitated a better breed of animals in British Columbia.[6] To realize maximum profit from any of his stock animals, he had to improve their quality, and he began to do just that in mid-1888. He purchased a purebred Durham Shorthorn cow and bull calf from a J.T. Steele, which would help him produce cattle of better quality.[7] No doubt he knew of "the tremendous ability of the Durham or Shorthorn breed of cattle to fatten quickly and well on grass."[8] While some area ranchers had preceded O'Keefe in breed enhancement, many other stock raisers followed suit the following year.

Hagan reported that Interior cattlemen wished to bring in "two or more carloads of desirable bulls" with which to improve the bloodlines of their cattle.[9] O'Keefe was a member of an elite group of local cattlemen who wished to restrict participation in the annual roundups of animals roaming the ranges and to resolve ownership. A roundup occurred each autumn, when farmers would go out to the summer ranges to retrieve their cows and any calves that had been born throughout the spring. In December 1889, O'Keefe was elected as a director of the British Columbia Cattle Association (BCCA), a position to which he was re-elected several times. The purpose of the association was to adopt "some very necessary rules" about how to conduct these roundups, as well as to settle "the many grievances from which stock raisers... [could] find no relief."[10] Some of these grievances were that cattle were allowed to roam freely from one pasture to another owned by someone else, or that a bull belonging to one owner had produced offspring with a cow belonging to a different owner; to whom would the calf belong? There were also issues regarding payment for the bulls' servicing of cows.

Those stock raisers who opted not to pay the BCCA's annual membership dues were excluded from participating in the yearly roundups. At the first annual general meeting of the BCCA, the members decided "to send to the Captain of each division immediately before each branding time a list of the members and the brands as recorded in the association books";[11] they planned to exclude anyone not on the list and to confiscate any cattle carrying brands not registered with the association. The exclusion of non-members was a way to ensure that the quality of members' herds would not be compromised by inferior animals. The BCCA instituted a system of a single annual roundup, at which they branded the cattle of all members within each of the various districts at the same time. They found that this system was

> very satisfactory and much cheaper than... the old system, while the cattle [were] benefited in the lesser amount of driving required for two brandings as compared with the system by which everyone went out to do his branding when it suited him best.[12]

The practice of branding livestock was not a new one; in fact, it dates back to as early as 2700 BC, as seen in Egyptian paintings

Cattle Baron to Land Baron

that depict marking animals with a hot iron. A definitive and permanent mark indicates ownership and deters theft. Branding was introduced in the New World by Hernando Cortez in 1541, when he "brought cattle stamped with his mark of three crosses." Branding animals with a distinctive mark made identification much easier, since "unbranded animals... [were] almost impossible to legally identify."[13]

Branding also simplified the buying and selling of livestock. In the case of multiple brands on an animal, a bill of sale had to be produced to avoid a potential accusation of cattle rustling. In the mid to late nineteenth century, the creation of an acceptable brand that could be used over a long period of time involved being able to fabricate it out of iron. The more intricate the brand, the more difficult it was to forge in iron, and the more difficult it was to get a clean brand without blotches. Therefore, most brands were simple ones, including O'Keefe's first: "11," which was registered on January 12, 1874. Indeed, he was the earliest in the area to register a brand. Other ranchers followed suit: C.A. Vernon in 1877; Price Ellison in 1893; and Thomas Wood in 1894.[14] The BC Express Company, Francis Jones Barnard, and O'Keefe all had their brands published in the *Inland Sentinel* on March 8, 1890. Either O'Keefe or his second wife, Elizabeth, later changed the "11" to an "O" with three lines to indicate a backward "K" attached at the left of the "O." This brand was published in the book BC *Horse and Cattle Brands* in 1924. Perhaps the old brand was too easy to duplicate or change, or perhaps they wanted one that reflected the family name.

Placement of the brand was also important. Cattle brands were usually on the ribs or shoulder, while on horses, it was more common on the shoulder (or occasionally the stifle). The method of branding cattle in those pioneer years involved heating the branding iron in a wood fire until the iron was the colour of ashes. A red-hot iron was too hot; the correct temperature would "burn the hair and the outer layer of skin."[15] A properly branded animal would be marked for the rest of its life. There was also a certain etiquette regarding the branding: no one was permitted to brand someone else's animal, and often only the actual owner or his foreman was allowed to place the iron on the stock animal.[16]

While cattle association members wanted to protect their herds from potential low-quality breeding stock, it is also likely that they wished to eliminate some of the competition from smaller stock raising operations. The anticipated shipment of "choice cattle" that Hagan mentioned arrived by steamer at Sicamous in May 1889, after a long journey from Quebec. Of the twenty-seven animals in the shipment, O'Keefe and Greenhow each took delivery of two Poll-Angus bulls, as did area ranchers A.L. Fortune, Lequime, and F.G. Vernon, while Luc Girouard, E.J. Tronson, and Thomas Wood each took only one. The price was "$225 each"—no small investment for any of the ranchers. The new breeding programs undertaken by these men were believed by many to be beneficial not only to the breeders, but also to the whole industry. Hagan summed up the public's attitude toward the programs by saying that "great credit [was] due to the enterprising parties who [had] thus nobly taken steps to improve the stock of the country."[17]

* * *

In addition to his membership in the BCCA, O'Keefe was a member of the Okanagan and Spallumcheen Agricultural Society, for which he was elected a director in 1891.[18] In 1887, O'Keefe was one

Cattle Baron to Land Baron

of several men who paced off a 1.6-kilometre racetrack for horse racing.[19] Had O'Keefe not been respected by the participants, it is doubtful that he would have been allowed to set the course with gentlemen such as E.J. Tronson and Price Ellison.[20] With his social standing secure, O'Keefe once again continued to enlarge his landholdings during the late 1880s.

Having more cattle meant that more land had to be obtained. Throughout the last years of the 1880s and into the next decade, O'Keefe made several more purchases. In 1888, he advertised in the *Inland Sentinel* his intention that in sixty days' time he planned "to apply to the Honourable Chief Commissioner of Lands and Works for permission to purchase 640 acres, more or less of pastoral lands" that bordered Okanagan Lake.[21] Only a few weeks later, Mary Ann advertised her intention to buy another 400 acres (162 hectares) to be used for pasturage.[22] This acreage adjoined the property to be purchased by her husband, and both properties adjoined or were adjacent to the land purchased from Greenhow in 1874. These 1888 acquisitions gave O'Keefe even more lakefront acreage for his exclusive use. In May of 1889, he made two more applications to purchase land; the first was for "294 acres of pastoral land... commencing at a post placed on the shore of Okanagan Lake, running west about 60 chains to a point at the edge of Okanagan Lake; thence following the meander of the Lake to the starting point." The second was for "514 acres... commencing at the north-west corner stake of Lot 65, Group 1, running west 80 chains; thence south 80 chains; thence east 40 chains; thence following the meander of Okanagan Lake to the south-west corner stake, Lot 65, Group 1; thence north to [the] starting point."[23]

Because of their proximity to water, these properties were extremely valuable. By the late 1880s, in addition to the acreages on Okanagan Lake, he and Greenhow owned much of the land surrounding Swan Lake, with the only exceptions being the small Indigenous reserve land at the north end of the lake and the sixty-five-hectare section on the west side owned by one H.S. Mason.

* * *

Just as O'Keefe was an entrepreneur in his own right, so was Greenhow. He was instrumental in bringing a steamer to Okanagan Lake in April of 1886; it was named after his daughter. This effort to improve transportation, an "important undertaking," was neither

> the work of the Government nor was it subsidized or assisted in any way by the Government, but was due wholly to the initiative and enterprise of two men, Captain J.D. Shorts and Thomas Greenhow... The vessel was the "Mary Victoria Greenhow."

The vessel's maiden voyage to Penticton became the source of much humour for Greenhow because the boat, with its "two horsepower coal-oil-burning engine," ran out of fuel before reaching Penticton. For the return trip, Captain Shorts managed to cajole people living along the lakeshore into parting with their supplies of the necessary fuel. Fortunately,

> Thomas Greenhow was blessed with a keen sense of humour, and if he lost money on the venture he appeared to get lots of fun out of it. In after years he could never tell of Short's trip down the lake when he ran short of coal oil, without going into roars of laughter.[24]

Cattle Baron to Land Baron

Greenhow's attitude toward earning or losing money was similar to that of O'Keefe, who, while not enjoying a losing venture, was still willing to risk some capital for a chance at financial gain. Buying and selling cattle, employing new (perhaps unproven) technology: that one must spend money to make money was something these entrepreneurs understood well.

* * *

O'Keefe also valued education. Because of his own relatively extensive education as a youngster in Ontario, O'Keefe knew his children would also benefit from going to a good school. To that end, in 1887, he sent two daughters, seven-year-old Nellie and six-year-old Lillie, to Notre-Dame du Sacré-Coeur Young Ladies Literary Institute in Ottawa. A boarding school education in those days was not cheap. Their room, board, and tuition for that year totalled $128.10, and the following year the amount was $125.10.[25] Their education did not end there; in 1905, O'Keefe sent them to Portland, Oregon, for "a course of training at St. Vincent's Hospital." A son, Leo, was sent to the University of Ottawa in 1906, and subsequently attended the University of Toronto, where he obtained a degree in law.[26] O'Keefe also sent three of the children he had with his second wife, Elizabeth, to school: Cornelius Jr. to the University of Toronto, and Margaret and Eileen to St. Ann's Academy in Victoria. While educating the children was expensive, O'Keefe no doubt was very proud of his children's academic accomplishments.

O'Keefe continued to increase his landholdings throughout the last decade of the nineteenth century. Early in 1890, he advertised his intention to apply for permission to purchase "the south half of Section 16, Township 8,"[27] comprising 129 hectares near Swan Lake; it was also adjacent to the property he would buy from Mason two years later. In 1891, O'Keefe published his intention to purchase 259 hectares near Okanagan Lake; the property adjoined land owned by Greenhow's widow and also bordered the land O'Keefe had bought from Greenhow in 1874.[28] Also in 1891, the *Vernon News* reported, "Mr. O'Keefe is erecting a house for his men and 300 feet of cattle sheds on his meadow near the race track. He expects to put up about 500 tons of hay this fall and winter 1,000 head of cattle."[29] The necessity of the cattle sheds and the bunkhouse, along with his ability to pay for them, meant that he was indeed a force to be reckoned with.

O'Keefe continued to take control of as much of the area around Swan Lake as possible. In early 1892, he bought an eight-hectare parcel along the lake.[30] Less than a month later, he purchased fifty hectares from Luc Girouard; the land had a small frontage on Okanagan Lake and adjoined the Indigenous reserve.[31] This small parcel also bordered the southern boundary of the property O'Keefe had bought from Greenhow eighteen years earlier. O'Keefe now possessed all the available land between the small reserve on the arm of Okanagan Lake (where present-day Kin Beach is) and the larger reserve on the northernmost arm of the lake. With such large tracts of land under his control, O'Keefe began to exert his rights of sole ownership by erecting fences. His plan to fence 809 hectares of pasture was announced in the *Vernon News*, which reported that the "nearly eight miles of Russell fence" would enclose the larger portion of his land adjoining the First Nation reserve on the east side of the lake's northernmost arm. By the early spring of 1892, O'Keefe had "fenced in the new

Cattle Baron to Land Baron

strip along Swan Lake and put it in wheat," which gave him "a straight three miles of wheat along the shore of the lake."[32] Fencing his property would prevent the bloodlines of his cattle from being diluted by inferior animals; it also kept cattle from grazing in his wheat fields.

* * *

O'Keefe continued to improve his breeding stock, not only in cattle, but also in pigs, sheep, and horses. In early 1892, he and Elizabeth Greenhow "purchased from Mr. J.T. Steele, [of] Salmon River, six thoroughbred Shorthorn bulls." By March of 1892, O'Keefe's cattle herd had grown to the extent that he was able to turn out to pasture "three hundred head of cattle on his range adjoining the commonage."[33] He also purchased more cattle to enlarge his herd, and in 1893, he bought three hundred "calves from the Coldstream ranch and removed them... to his corrals near Swan Lake," probably to fatten them up so he could sell them at a profit a few months later. O'Keefe's desire to improve his pigs and sheep is shown by his purchase of "a thoroughbred Chester white boar... and a Southdown ram" from Salmon Arm resident J.B. Graves; the purchase was seen as an "important addition to the live stock of the district."[34]

Because O'Keefe was also interested in improving the lineage of his draft horses, he purchased the breeding services of a registered thoroughbred Shire stallion in the spring of 1893. Described as a "heavy draft" horse that weighed 1900 pounds and stood over seventeen hands high, "and very well got up throughout," the horse was "much superior to any heavy draft that ever travelled over [the Okanagan] route." Area ranchers were exhorted to secure his stud services and to "raise a class of horses" that would "supply the coast market for heavy draying purposes."[35]

O'Keefe was not the only rancher who sought to improve the quality his livestock. Price Ellison purchased an English Shire stallion, "Grove Traction," in 1892, and advertised him at stud. Ellison also shared with O'Keefe an interest in new machinery. He had "the right of sale" of a "new machine for building the Kitselman wire fence" that "weaves the meshes upon wires strung horizontally along posts."[36] This was an ingenious mechanism comprising a series of reels with wire rolled onto them; as the machine was moved along a fence line, the operator would use a handle to turn the reels; they in turn would string and twist the wire vertically on the horizontal wires. Because the spaces between the wires were quite small, the fence was effective in preventing predators from entering the area, thereby protecting the cattle or other livestock enclosed within—an important consideration given that the cattlemen continued improving the quality of their stock.

With many of the area's stock raisers involved in improving their animal breeds, the Okanagan and Spallumcheen Agricultural Society began holding annual fall exhibitions at which farmers could display their animals and compete for prizes. The first exhibition was held in 1891, and O'Keefe took second place for his Hereford calf, first place for his two-year-old heifer, and second place in the "general purpose horse" division for his two-year-old horse.[37]

By 1893, O'Keefe's efforts to improve his line of pigs paid off when he won first place for his Chester White sow—no doubt the offspring of the boar bought in 1892. He also won second prizes for his Hereford cow and calf, his Durham Shorthorn cow and calf,

Cattle Baron to Land Baron

and his pair of carriage horses under 15.5 hands. In 1894, O'Keefe had better results, taking first-place honours for his yearling Chester White boar (probably another product of the purebred boar), and for his Hereford bull, milk cow, and yearling heifer.[38]

* * *

While O'Keefe was clearly interested in improving the bloodlines of his farm animals, he was also responsive to the burgeoning styles and technologies of the day, because he knew that in employing such modern innovations he would be able to increase the overall production of his ranching operation, which would in turn enable him to make some home improvements. His purchases indicate that O'Keefe was a man who wanted the best of everything that his money could buy. In 1896, O'Keefe erected "a large windmill of a most modern type" with which water was pumped from Deep Creek to his house.[39] Also in 1896, he decided to build a second addition on his house to accommodate his growing family. He secured the services of R.B. Bell, a local architect. Prior to moving to Vernon, Bell lived in Ottawa and had "worked on the construction of the Parliament buildings [and] helped to build the large doors in the west block and the speaker's chair in the House of Commons." As if that were not enough to establish a strong reputation as a master builder, Bell also worked on "St. Mary's Hospital, at New Westminster [and] ... also worked on the Vancouver Court House."[40] O'Keefe knew what he was doing in hiring Bell as his contractor, but perhaps there was another reason for hiring Bell.

In the late 1880s, Elizabeth Greenhow, whose husband died before he could build their new home, decided to go ahead with their plans. She engaged R.B. Bell to build the house, which

The Greenhow house.
COURTESY OF THE HISTORIC O'KEEFE RANCH

fulfilled her late husband's wishes.[41] The *Vernon News* reported on March 17, 1892, that

> Mrs. E. Greenhow is about to erect on the site of her present house what will be the finest residence in the valley. It will be a two-storey building... The cost will be between $6,000 and $7,000.

The new Greenhow home that Bell built had three stories, like the first extension on the O'Keefe log house. Unlike the O'Keefe home, however, the third floor of the Greenhow house was occasionally used as a dance floor. The house also featured bay windows

Cattle Baron to Land Baron

on both the first and second floors, a veranda on one side, and a small balcony above the front entrance. Unfortunately, this building burned down in 1939.

Considering that Elizabeth had recently employed Bell to design her beautiful new home, which was only a few metres from O'Keefe's, it would have been natural for O'Keefe to choose to use the same designer. Her home and the addition Bell designed for O'Keefe were among Bell's first projects after arriving in Vernon. However, Elizabeth Greenhow's new home was larger than the O'Keefe family home, and perhaps this sparked O'Keefe's desire to build an addition to his already lovely house, and also to use the same architect. According to an O'Keefe family story, there had always been some rivalry between O'Keefe and Greenhow. In an interview, Tierney O'Keefe, Cornelius's youngest son, said that "Mrs. Greenhow built a huge home, larger than this [O'Keefe] mansion, twenty-one rooms in it, and they were both wider, longer, and higher than rooms in this house. Friendly rivally [sic] shall I say."[42] It seems that Cornelius O'Keefe's somewhat competitive nature was well known to his youngest son. In fact, the *Vernon News* stated that when the second addition to the O'Keefe house was finished, the house would be "one of the finest (if not the finest) in the upper country."

The estimates from the several tenders for construction that O'Keefe received ranged from $9,500 to $12,000, no small sums in 1892, and almost twice the cost of building the entire new Greenhow home.[43] The average cost in those days of building a two-storey home ranged from $3,000 to $6,000,[44] depending on square footage and whether or not a furnace was installed; it is reasonable to assume that the 1896 renovation to the O'Keefes' home

Second addition to the log house, 1896. Note the lighter shade of shingles, indicating the new section.
COURTESY OF THE VERNON MUSEUM AND ARCHIVES

was higher than this price range, given that the new construction, which doubled the size of the house, was an addition to the 1886 renovation on the original log house built prior to 1877, because building additions to existing structures usually presented more difficulties than simply building new constructions.

To prepare for this 1896 addition, Bell and his partner, R.O. Constant, detached and moved the original log house to a different location, leaving the first addition of the parlour, den, and extra bedrooms, and in its place added a dining room, a larger kitchen, and several rooms on the second floor, giving the home a total of fourteen rooms. O'Keefe's choice of builder proved to be a good one. A photograph from 1896 shows a roof with two shades of shingles, the lighter shade indicating the new addition. The *Vernon News* was of the opinion, early in 1896, that the renovation would "make it one of the finest residences in the Interior";[45] this new addition apparently ended any competition between O'Keefe and Elizabeth Greenhow.[46]

* * *

The architect, Bell, was a busy man in the area. The December 6, 1894, edition of the *Vernon News* reported that Bell would be the contractor for a new hotel in Lumby. Bell's architectural firm also designed a number of other buildings, many of which still stand today, more than one hundred years later: the United Church rectory in Vernon on Twenty-Sixth Street at a cost of $4,500; the Herry home on what is now Barker Road in the BX area; the Gordon Robinson residence, which became Edgehill Manor;[47] the S.C. Smith house on Thirty-Second Avenue, which is now the Vernon Community Music School; and the home of W.E. Megaw, the well-known local proprietor of Megaw's Store. In 1910, Bell built a home on the shore of Kalamalka Lake for the local Buchanan family, for whom Buchanan Road in Coldstream was named.[48] Bell also worked on the Kalamalka Hotel, and "drew up the plans for City Hall and the Fire Hall."[49] The Fire Hall was torn down in 1951. Additionally, Bell and Constant were the superintendents for the construction of the Bank of Montreal and the bank manager's house.[50]

That most of these buildings are still standing strong is a testament to Bell and Constant's architectural innovation and integrity—qualities that O'Keefe admired. And O'Keefe was proud of the result, as the family regularly invited people to their home to see the renovations. The O'Keefe family said that the large, bright, and airy second-storey bedroom above the parlour was always kept for guests because it was the nicest of all the bedrooms. This kind of endorsement from a well-respected rancher and businessman would have helped Bell obtain other lucrative contracts, so it is likely the O'Keefe house became a model and a standard for other homes in the area.

The house hosted social evenings that are easy to imagine, given the items remaining in the house, and given the stories told by the family. At one dinner party, the story goes, the guests and their hosts were enjoying a meal in the dining room. Servers, specially employed for the occasion, attended to the guests' every need, refilling wine glasses, replenishing the various platters and bowls, and clearing the table of used crockery, stemware, and cutlery. The table would have been set with the best china, as well as the beautiful sterling silver cutlery given to Mary Ann by her husband. Everyone was having a grand evening, pleased to have been invited to one of the O'Keefes' well-known soirées.

Meanwhile, the children were spending their post-dinner evening in their bedrooms or the schoolroom, working on lessons, reading, or playing. Two of the girls, Margaret and Mary, who were around ten or twelve years of age, were occupied by something that became a family legend. The banister in the breakfast room had always held a particular fascination for the O'Keefe children, and the girls wasted no time in taking advantage of the relative freedom afforded by the adults' party going on around the corner. Perhaps they hoped that the dinner conversation would mask their squeals of delight as they took turns sliding down the banister. Whether going down facing forward or backward, they

Cattle Baron to Land Baron

could slow their descent by placing a foot on each stair tread as they slid. At the end of the banister was a newel post with a fairly large knob on the top, and the trick to avoiding getting caught on it was to place ones' hands on it and jump over it to the floor. On one particular trip, Margaret did not execute the slide perfectly. Perhaps she dragged her foot too much on the stair, or she caught it between the railing's supporting posts, or she missed the final jump over the newel post, or maybe her long dress or nightgown got tangled around her feet and legs. In any case, she fell, landing hard on the wooden chair at the bottom of the stairs and hitting her head in the process. She cut her head and may have been briefly knocked out.

Her sister's screams alerted their parents and guests and brought the whole party to an abrupt halt. The dinner guests were quickly ushered out so that she could be rushed by horse and buggy to the hospital, where she was stitched up.[51] She recovered nicely, and perhaps never tried sliding down the banister again. However, given the indented spot on each stair tread that is still evident today, her mishap did little to deter subsequent O'Keefe children from doing the same thing.

* * *

The improvements to his home and ranch, all within a few years, demonstrate how prosperous O'Keefe had become. He was considered one of the Okanagan's foremost pioneers, respected by most people in the area. Hagan said both O'Keefe and Greenhow were "recognized as land-marks in the district where they live, and their prosperity gives general pleasure."[52] O'Keefe was included in a photograph of a group of men called the "Fathers of the Okanagan," all of whom were well known in the Okanagan Valley. Also in the photograph are E.J. Tronson, Moses Lumby, Thomas Ellis, and Luc Girouard.

O'Keefe was generally well liked and trusted by his neighbours, friends, and acquaintances. In 1893, he was involved in an accident in which a horse kicked him in the head, and the attending doctor "was besieged with enquiries from the many friends of the genial rancher, and much relief was expressed when it was known that the patient was in no danger."[53] The brother of Luc Girouard, who had appointed O'Keefe as co-executor with W.F. Cameron, of Girouard's estate, attested to O'Keefe's honesty when he said, "heirs under their protection... are as safe as in a fire-proof safe."[54]

While he had earned the respect and affection of most people, O'Keefe had a reputation for being somewhat eccentric. Charlie Shaw, one of O'Keefe's employees, related a story about O'Keefe appreciating a rainfall. He said that O'Keefe "was just looking up, and it was sprinkling rain... It had been a dry spell for about three weeks." Then Shaw heard him say, "Thousands of dollars! Thousands of dollars! Thousands of dollars!"[55]

Another O'Keefe employee, George J. Fraser, told a story about O'Keefe's frugality. In the 1890s, when several men spent the winter feeding O'Keefe's cattle in the meadow, the cook discovered that one of the men would not eat potatoes. He asked O'Keefe to supply some beans so the man in question would have something fairly substantial to eat. O'Keefe did, indeed, take the men some beans to cook, "but he must have swept them from some old barn or granary floor for among the beans and dust [they] found shingle nails, bluestone and other odds and ends." Nevertheless, the cook served the beans every day, and when they ran out, O'Keefe was

Cattle Baron to Land Baron

Okanagan pioneers. Seated, left to right: E.J. Tronson, Bernard Lequime, Frederick Brent, I. Boucherie, and Thomas Ellis. Standing, left to right: Cornelius O'Keefe, Moses Lumby, Luc Girouard, and James Crozier. The photo was taken by A.D. Worgan, ca. 1890, and it became part of Mrs. N.L. Pottie's collection. It was published on October 21, 1937, in the "Okanagan Marching Forward: Special Edition" of the *Vernon News*, in an article by Margaret Ormsby entitled "The City of Vernon Salutes Its Pioneers" (p. 21).
COURTESY OF THE VERNON MUSEUM AND ARCHIVES

asked to get some more. When they ran out a second time, O'Keefe told the cook that he would have to raise some on the farm, and by the time they ran out of beans for the third time, "the cattle were on the range," suggesting his thriftiness: the sooner the cattle were out on the range, finding their own feed, the sooner he could stop purchasing beans for the men because they no longer had to stay on the ranch to feed the cattle. But even though he was frugal, "Connie was a splendid man to work for," said Fraser. O'Keefe, he went on, "never had a foreman and he never got out to the fields to see how the work was progressing," because there was "a splendid spirit of co-operation among the men" and "a natural placement of work on the basis of seniority... The plan worked well at O'Keefe's but one can well visualize conditions where it would not."[56]

He seemed to engender loyalty and hard work among his employees, but according to Fraser, O'Keefe had another eccentricity: he tended to cut the monthly wages of his employees without informing them of his intentions. Generally, they would find less money in their pay packet, and although "they did not like his method of making the cut... they thought they had better swallow their pride and keep their jobs. They would never find a better place to work and the pay they had received was the generally going wage." They believed their boss to be a good and fair one. Occasionally, O'Keefe paid wages for very little work; his employees thought these actions were peculiar. Fraser recalled that he had been hired for a specific job that would not actually begin for another month, so he spent that month "killing time with the boys" and did nothing to earn those wages. O'Keefe was known, Fraser said, "to do things that would not make sense with anybody else but the pay was sure nevertheless."[57] Charlie Shaw described O'Keefe as "quite a cattleman," "very miserly with his help. He was a stubborn little Irishman."[58] Fraser went on to say that "O'Keefe was surely an odd character," and that "more interesting tales [were] told of Connie than of any other of the old timers of the Okanagan."[59] Another story, told by Catherine Neave, Tierney O'Keefe's mother-in-law, illustrates O'Keefe's sense of "justice":

Cattle Baron to Land Baron

One man asked what time they would get up in the morning to go to work, and O'Keefe said, "When the rooster crows." One decided to crow about midnight. So the boss got the men up and they started for the woods. They drove for hours before the daylight came. That rooster wasn't around for very many more breakfasts.[60]

O'Keefe's intemperate nature was shown on July 2, 1897, when he was charged with assault, but the charge was dismissed.[61] Although O'Keefe's employees appeared to enjoy working for him, Fraser said that O'Keefe had a

> very noticeable peculiarity... He was very likely to fly into a rage and cuss a man for carelessness when a trifling accident such as the breaking of a whiffle tree would be brought to his attention, while in the case of losing a good horse in a runaway, all he said was "too many oats."[62]

Even though O'Keefe was rather unsophisticated, his eccentricities did not seem to have hurt his reputation, because his good name remained intact. He became known as

> The O'Keefe of Okanagan, pronouncing the last word as if it rhymed with Finnegan or Flannigan. There was nothing nasty or malicious about it because... Mr. O'Keefe,... although of Irish decent [sic], a wealthy stock raiser and a genial, kindly man, was well liked and respected by everyone... [and] a lot of [his neighbours, such as] George and Charles Vernon,... Tronson,... and others, all Irish, appreciated [this title].[63]

This custom of adding "the" before a person's name had come from Ireland, where each clan elected a leader who was then referred to as "the O'Dowd" or "the O'Flaherty." Their descendants retained the title, so the custom of assigning a title was not a new one for the Irish in Canada. Although the Anglo-Irish in the area might have thought the expression was pretentious, and therefore more of a joke than a compliment, O'Keefe chose to accept it as a tribute because he was proud of his Irish heritage and believed he had earned the title as a sign of respect. The qualification "although of Irish decent [sic]"[64] indicates that the writer thought that people respected O'Keefe in spite of his ethnic background; it also suggests that the author considered others of Irish descent to be unworthy of such esteem. Regardless of either O'Keefe's ethnic heritage or his occasional eccentric behaviour, O'Keefe's reputation as a leading pioneer and businessman continued to grow.

In 1894, O'Keefe was elected president of the Vernon Jockey Club. This election came after he offered to sell 1.6 hectares of his property to the Okanagan and Spallumcheen Agricultural Society for the purpose of creating a racetrack. He proposed to sell the land "and lease the present race track or a portion of ground equal to it in size for a term of from 1 to 5 years." After O'Keefe's election as Jockey Club president, he

> reported that he was prepared to let the Society have another acre of land at the same price paid for their first purchase... and further hinted that there was no immediate necessity for the payment... and a motion was passed accepting his proposal.[65]

Cattle Baron to Land Baron

Perhaps it is no coincidence that he was elected after his offer to sell the land at a reasonable price, and once his position was assured, he offered another acre for sale. His awareness of the status afforded by the presidency of such a club was no doubt the result of his early years in Ontario, where membership in hunt or jockey clubs ensured a high social position.

* * *

O'Keefe may not have aspired to political life himself, other than through his memberships in various community organizations, but he was not averse to becoming politically active. On the first page of the June 2, 1898, edition of the *Vernon News*, it was reported that "O'Keefe was a delegate at the convention to select a government candidate for the East Yale Riding," at which "Price Ellison was unanimously selected to be the candidate in the upcoming provincial election." Ellison went on to win that election and several others thereafter, and became the chief commissioner of lands and works in 1909, and then the provincial minister of finance and agriculture in 1910.[66] Ellison had arrived in British Columbia in 1876, when he quickly made a name for himself. He opened "the first blacksmith shop south of Kamloops, and was the first to grow wheat in the bush land in the Interior without irrigation." He also had "a four-year contract, with the Dominion Government, to convey the mails from Sicamous to Vernon and Okanagan Mission."[67]

Like O'Keefe, Ellison built a log cabin to live in,[68] and he was a visionary in terms of what he thought he could achieve, again similar to O'Keefe. According to one of Ellison's daughters, upon his arrival in the area, he said to his companions, "Boys, I am going no further; this is my dream. I see gold in the rocks, cattle on the hill-sides, orchards on the benches and beauty everywhere."[69] This sentiment echoes that of O'Keefe when he and his partners chose to settle at the Head of the Lake in 1867; O'Keefe also "saw" what could become of the land. Also, like O'Keefe, Ellison clearly knew how to conduct business: "he learned to speak the Chinook language used by early traders dealing with the Indians."[70] However, his employees apparently liked him better. Another daughter said that Ellison "was greatly loved and respected by his men. His attitude to them was generous and fair minded and kindly."[71]

Having been instrumental in Ellison's initial political success was surely a feather in O'Keefe's cap, as the two were also friends and business associates. In fact they, along with E.J. Tronson, sought to incorporate 25,710 hectares of land into a municipality known as "The Corporation of the District of Okanagan,"[72] but there is no subsequent evidence that their application was taken seriously. This land would have included much of Vernon and the surrounding area.

O'Keefe was attuned to the production value of his land. He planted an orchard that the *Vernon News* said had "splendid apples of the wealthy variety... [that] would be hard to beat in any country, and were much admired by all who saw them."[73] He also knew that the coming of the railway would have an impact on grain farmers, and he made considerable efforts to produce more grain. The railway, Hagan observed in 1891, would provide both "a market as well as facilities for handling the grain, so... farmers were confident in expecting a larger harvest the following year."[74] During spring ploughing in 1892, the *Vernon News* reported that there were "no less than ten ploughs... working on

Mr. O'Keefe's ranches." By June of the same year, O'Keefe had sown "six hundred acres of spring wheat and sixty of oats," and he had "over three hundred acres... in summer fallow." After the 1892 fall harvest, the newspaper reported O'Keefe's great demand for railway transport: "all the spare cars that [could] be procured [were] being used... in the shipment of wheat by Mr. O'Keefe and the BX Ranch." The following week it remarked again on the large size of wheat shipments, with "Lord Aberdeen's Coldstream ranch and those of O'Keefe and Mrs. Greenhow... using most of the spare cars."[75]

With all the planting and ploughing being done on O'Keefe's ranch, it is no wonder that his equipment started to need repairs. The machinery purchased in 1888 was initially quite expensive and of good quality and served O'Keefe well until 1894, when the binder and seed drill needed repairs. That year, a bill for parts for his cultivator, drill, Brantford binder, mower knife, and ploughs totalled $63.75.[76] That same spring, O'Keefe advertised for sale "about thirty tons [of] first-class oats, suitable for feed or seed oats,"[77] a sign that he was planting and harvesting large amounts of grain. He was also shipping considerable quantities of grain to the Columbia Milling Company. Between February 13 and March 8, 1894, he shipped at least 2,400 sacks of wheat, using five rail cars; the year's income from wheat alone was over $1,900.[78] If O'Keefe's shipments are any indication of the extent to which the railway was being used, then both his and Hagan's predictions of its impact were proven to be true.

Perhaps because he was shipping fairly large quantities of wheat to a milling company, and because he saw an opportunity to make some more money, O'Keefe took out shares in the

Okanagan Flouring Mills Company Limited, a company registered in September of 1895; its "capital stock was $60,000 divided into 600 shares at $100 each," and the registered shareholders included Cornelius O'Keefe. The mill was in working order within a year, and for about ten years "was quite successful." By 1900, with competition from the prairies heating up, the company began to lose business, so the shareholders chose to "wind up the affairs of the company." The original five directors, including O'Keefe, were each told to pay $7,000 to the bank within the year, and the sum, "on competent advice, was paid."[79] This was probably less than each actually owed, but the bank chose to be magnanimous.

* * *

Although O'Keefe owned hundreds of acres on which he grazed his cattle and planted and harvested grain and apples, he continued to buy land into the 1890s. He also continued his association with J.B. Greaves; in March of 1895, Greaves purchased "nearly a thousand head of stock" from O'Keefe, Mrs. Greenhow, and others.[80] In 1896, O'Keefe purchased two more acreages, one from William Ward Spinks and the other from H.S. Mason. Both properties bordered land that O'Keefe already owned, and both had frontage along Swan Lake. The land bought from Spinks comprised thirty-five hectares in the southwest quarter of Section 15, Township 8, and the north half of Section 10, Township 8, and cost $870.[81] The purchase from Mason was the northwest quarter of Section 15, Township 8, and carried a price tag of $580.[82] O'Keefe had no qualms about paying as much as $100 per acre for good bottomland because he knew that without exclusive access to water,

Cattle Baron to Land Baron

very little of his farming and ranching operation could survive for long. Two years later, he purchased a new threshing machine, the "Toronto Advance," the first of the kind in the district; it did "away with the labour of several men."[83] Again, although the new machinery was expensive, O'Keefe knew that in the long run it would save him much in the way of labourers' wages, increasing his profit and demonstrating that he was a progressive farmer.

O'Keefe's purchases of livestock and land, his affinity for new technologies, and his various appointments all served to enhance his reputation as an astute businessman and as a member of the social elite of the North Okanagan area. He continued to invest in other ventures, as we will see in the next chapter.

CHAPTER

10

Marriage, Mining, and Milling

IN LATE 1898, Mary Ann O'Keefe suffered a stroke from which she never recovered, and on January 30, 1899, she died at the age of forty-nine, leaving eight children.[1] The obituary on the front page of the paper was full of praise for both her and her husband. She had been closely connected, it said, "with much that is best in the history of the district"; her death left a gap that would only "with difficulty be filled."[2] The obituary noted that her husband was "one of the most prominent ranchers and wheat growers in the province," with extensive connections, which "afforded to Mrs. O'Keefe an opportunity to control a large sphere of influence."[3] Alice Barrett Parke, whose husband managed the BX Ranch, wrote in her journal that "Mrs. O'Keefe was a good mother and a good friend," who "will be very much missed & mourned."[4] Because of O'Keefe's prominence, the funeral was attended by several of

Marriage, Mining, and Milling

the area's important citizens, including "pall bearers A.L. Fortune, Capt. Cumming, G.A. Henderson, E.J. Tronson, W.F. Cameron, [and] T. Clinton."[5]

Later that same year, O'Keefe travelled to Ontario to make arrangements for the wedding of one of his daughters. There he met his second wife, Elizabeth Tierney, the sister of the groom. At twenty-three years of age, she was forty years his junior. Her family was well respected and prosperous in the Ottawa area, with some members having appeared "on council and on the magistrates bench after [the] mid-[nineteenth] century."[6] Her father was James Tierney, and her grandfather was Denis Tierney Sr., an early Irish settler in the township.[7] Elizabeth was well educated and able to cope with the social demands of a well-respected farmer such as O'Keefe. In addition, she was a talented artist. Two of her paintings are on display in the O'Keefe mansion, one in the den of the mansion and the other in the dining room. Both are testament to Elizabeth's considerable artistic talent.

When O'Keefe and Elizabeth met, she was contemplating becoming a nun, which may be why she was not yet married. Her son Tierney mentions that she also had what he called a wandering eye. Why she changed her mind about becoming a nun is unknown. Perhaps she was intrigued by this rancher from the wilds of British Columbia, or maybe she felt sorry for the widower with eight children; she may have felt unsure of her choice to become a nun, or perhaps she simply fell in love with O'Keefe. In any case, she consented to his marriage proposal and moved west after their wedding.

The photograph of her, taken around the time of the wedding, shows a pretty woman with large eyes. Her hair is attractively

Elizabeth Tierney O'Keefe, ca. 1900.
COURTESY OF THE HISTORIC O'KEEFE RANCH

styled, and her clothing is appropriate for a genteel young woman. Her dress appears to be made of satin or perhaps taffeta, with the bodice and sleeves pin-tucked; in addition, the bodice has some decorative ruching. She has a beautiful brooch at her throat and a fleur-de-lis pin on her tie, which is made of the same fabric as her blouse and is edged with satin cord. (Were the brooch and the tiepin gifts from O'Keefe? The latter would have been a reminder of his mother's French heritage.)

When Elizabeth married O'Keefe in 1900, she inherited a family of eight children, including a stepson, Charles, who at twenty-two was only one year her junior. O'Keefe was already sixty-three in 1900, and in 1901, Elizabeth gave birth to the first

Marriage, Mining, and Milling

of six children; the last one was born when he was seventy-five. It is likely that he loved her very much. He bought her a beautiful set of sterling silver cutlery (which is still in the mansion) for the household. The cutlery, along with a large wooden chest, was bought from Birks Jewellers in Ottawa and shipped west around 1901, perhaps to commemorate the birth of their first child. The set includes fish knives (and other knives for various purposes), serving spoons, sugar shells, meat forks, and of course the usual forks, knives, and spoons. There are twelve place settings, and the handle of each piece is elaborately engraved with Elizabeth O'Keefe's initials.[8] Their marriage lasted until O'Keefe's death in 1919.

Elizabeth earned a fine reputation in her own right, as she continued the charity work started by her predecessor, Mary Ann. In 1902, Elizabeth O'Keefe and Elizabeth Greenhow were elected to the executive of the local chapter of the Women's National Council, and in 1905, both women were elected to the Vernon Jubilee Hospital Board of Directors. Elizabeth also continued Mary Ann's work with the church; in 1902, she helped to raise funds to purchase a new bronze bell for St. James Catholic Church, which was blessed by Bishop Dontonville and "named Elizabeth in honor of Mrs. O'Keefe, who was chiefly instrumental in securing the bell, it being owing to her energetic efforts that the subscription was circulated."[9]

* * *

As was evident in other aspects of O'Keefe's life, he knew that financial success lay in the diversification and sometimes the liquidation of his assets. In 1896, he became a stockholder in the Silver Queen Mining Company (later changed to the Silver Star Mining Company), which was relatively successful. This mine was located on what was then called Aberdeen Mountain (later renamed Silver Star Mountain), east of Vernon. In March of 1897, the newspaper reported that at "the first general meeting of the shareholders of the Silver Star mine,... five directors were elected for the ensuing year: C. O'Keefe, A.G. Fuller, A.J. McMullen, W.E. Ellis... [and] Evan Perry." Only two months later, the paper stated that an employee of the mine had taken in "some specimens of galena" from the mine "which would gladden the eyes of the most exacting mining expert." The ore appeared to be "fully as good as anything from the Slocan district... [and] a recent assay... went 100 ounces in silver and $3.20 in gold." In 1899, the newspaper reported that an important mining deal had been concluded that week, whereby the rich property of the Silver Star Mining Company had been bonded to an English company for the sum of $30,000." Furthermore, the 1902 Minister of Mines Report stated that the mine carried "galena with iron and copper pyrites, and assaying $100 per ton in silver and gold."[10] These reports are evidence that, at least in the short term, O'Keefe and his mining partners were finding some success in the business.

O'Keefe was also a partner in the Clara and Corrine mineral claim at Round Lake.[11] This claim was said to be among "the most promising of claims in the district";[12] just a month later, a representative of a mining syndicate from Vancouver inspected the site and "was much pleased with the appearance of the claim, and... entered into negotiations for its purchase." The representative believed that "the ore from [the claim] and the Silver Star would be treated by the Tocoma [sic] smelter without charge as it would serve admirably for fluxing purposes."[13] On May 27, 1897, the *Vernon News* reported that "W.A. Carlyle, the well-known Provincial

Marriage, Mining, and Milling

Mineralogist," "was particularly impressed with the galena ore shown him from the Silver Star" because it was "very similar to the famous silver-producing ores of the Slocan district. He advised the owners "to vigorously prosecute work" on the claim. O'Keefe and his partners were "on the right track"—at least as far as this particular mine was concerned.

Besides Silver Star and Clara and Corrine, O'Keefe was involved with another mineral claim, this one situated "on the west side of Okanagan Lake... about two-and-a-half miles west of the Head of the Lake, close to the Indian reserve," called the Iron Point; its "croppings [were] assaying $10.90 gold, besides silver and copper."[14] Not two months later, the paper reported that yet another mineral claim, this time thirteen kilometres east of Vernon, had been recorded by A.G. Fuller, A.J. McMullen, C. O'Keefe, and A. Clark; this one was called the Mountain Lion. Clearly, O'Keefe was not one to let moss grow under his feet; he saw opportunities in many different ventures and did not hesitate to take advantage of them.

O'Keefe continued to produce large quantities of wheat, and subscribed to $2,000 worth of shares in the Okanagan Flour Milling Company Limited, which commenced operations in 1896, and which operated quite successfully for several years. Instead of selling his wheat and allowing someone else to profit from the processing of the grain, O'Keefe saw the potential for increased profit if he held shares in a milling operation. Unfortunately, because the company was forced to import certain varieties of wheat from Manitoba and the North-West Territories to mix with the varieties produced in the Okanagan, production costs became prohibitive and forced the company to declare bankruptcy in 1906.

***

By 1904, with real estate prices rising, O'Keefe began selling his property. The increased competition in the cattle market drove cattle prices down, and people wanted land for purposes other than raising stock. In February 1904, he advertised his land between Vernon and Okanagan Landing, considered to be good bench and bottomland with ample water, for an average price of $50 per acre. He would sell it in blocks to suit purchasers. The advertisement was repeated in the April 7, 1904, edition of the newspaper. In August of that year, O'Keefe purchased four-tenths of an acre (0.2 hectares) in the northeast and northwest quarters of Section 3, Township 8 for $75. Although this seems like a high price to pay for less than an acre, his plan became evident in his later sale of part of this land for $100. O'Keefe sold land in both large and small parcels; in December 1904, he sold 1,185.09 acres (480 hectares) to a Samuel Polson for a total of $59,254 (or slightly less than $50 per acre), and two years later he subdivided 400 acres (162 hectares) with frontage on Swan Lake into ten- and twenty-acre (four- and eight-hectare) lots. Also in 1906, O'Keefe sold twenty acres (eight hectares) at $135 per acre to a man named George Harper, who wanted to plant fruit trees.

O'Keefe also held mortgages on land that he had sold. In an undated statement of mortgages and cash received on deals after December 15, 1905 (Table 1), the amounts already received totalled $14,263.48.[15] He did not sell the land because he needed the money immediately, but rather because he saw the value of a regular income from mortgage payments. In 1907, six of the children O'Keefe had with Mary Ann relinquished their ownership of the land left to them by their mother and turned it over to their

Marriage, Mining, and Milling

Mortgagee	Acres	Rate/ acre ($)	Total cost of land ($)	Mortgages held by O'Keefe ($)	Cash received by O'Keefe ($)
Taylor	20.00	75	1,500	1,000.00	333.33
Purdon	10.00	75	750	500.00	166.66
Hatch	23.00	80	1,840	1,226.67	383.33
Brisbin	20.91	80	1,673	1,115.33	348.50
Elliott	23.00	80	1,760	1,173.34	366.66
Hilliard	10.00	75	750	500.00	166.66
Wilson	5.00	-	300	-	-
McCutcheon	10.00	80	800	533.34	166.66
Smith	10.00	80	800	533.34	166.66
McDowell	19.25	100	1,925	1,259.00	569.00
Fear	17.05	100	1,705	505.00	1000.00
				$8,346.02	$3,917.46
			Cash already paid:		$2,000.00
			Total mortgages held by O'Keefe:		$8,346.02
		Total amount received in mortgages and cash:			$14,263.48
		Amount due to make up ⅓: 19,751.33 - 14,263.48 = $5,487.85			
		Deals unfinished: Graham, $1,120, and Wylie, $2,450			

Table 1. Mortgages held and cash received by Cornelius after December 15, 1905. FROM A DOCUMENT IN THE O'KEEFE FAMILY ARCHIVES (BOX 4), HISTORIC O'KEEFE RANCH

father for the sum of one dollar. Mary Ann had purchased the land in 1888 and 1889; it adjoined the land that O'Keefe had bought from Greenhow in 1886. A large map from the Historic Ranch archives shows O'Keefe's landholdings as of April 1907, and differentiates between Greenhow's real estate and O'Keefe's original pre-emption. This map does not represent the full extent of his landholdings prior to 1907, and any properties sold prior to that year are not indicated.[16]

O'Keefe's plan for land sales became evident in December 1907, when he completed a huge sale of property to the Land and Agriculture Company of Canada. The sale comprised approximately 5,700 acres (2,307 hectares) and netted him $184,193 (or about $32.31 per acre). The newspaper reported that "the magnitude of the transaction" eclipsed "any previous change of ownership in the Okanagan district." The sum at that time was considered to be a fortune. In April of 1913 he gave the city of Vernon an option to buy fifty acres (twenty hectares) in the city for $32,000 (or $640 per acre), providing a good profit over what he had paid for it.

Approximately eighty-one hectares of O'Keefe's property remained, upon which stood his house, the church, and other buildings, and which remained in the family for a number of years.[17]

CHAPTER

11

Technology and Other Amenities

O'KEEFE'S INVOLVEMENT IN diverse ventures and the liquidation of much of his real estate made it possible for him to improve his home. The added modern amenities included a furnace, running water, indoor plumbing, hardwood flooring, and new furniture. In 1907, he was one of the first in the area to install a telephone, but this sign of progress also proved to be the source of tragedy.

In 1910, his son, Charles (eldest son of Mary Ann), was killed while riding his horse in Vernon on December 20. A coroner's inquest was held; however,

> little light was thrown upon the sad occurrence, but it [was] regarded that Mr. O'Keefe lost his hat, and while stooping from the saddle to recover it, the horse swerved, bringing his head into contact with the telephone pole on which were found

marks of blood... [The] verdict:... the cause of his death was fracture of the skull.[1]

The funeral was held on December 29, with interment in the family cemetery.[2]

Earlier that year, O'Keefe had installed a furnace that was guaranteed in even the coldest weather to heat the two main floors of the house to a minimum temperature of sixty-five degrees Fahrenheit. Running water and indoor plumbing were installed at the same time. The cost for the Pease-Waldon Company to install the Florence boiler, pipes, overflow pipe, and expansion tank for hot water was $1,797.50—less than one percent of the profit from the 1907 land deal, but a small fortune for the time. Imagine the task of retrofitting a house with heating pipes between floors; not only would the installers have to figure out the best routes for the pipes, they would also have to deal with the building materials: plaster ceilings and walls, wood plank floors, and various wallpapers.[3] Also in 1910, the O'Keefes installed hardwood floors.

The following year, they purchased a new dining room suite, consisting of a table with six leaves, twelve chairs, a sideboard, a china cabinet, and a small side table, all for $399.70. This amount represented over a year's wages for the average cowboy at the time, who earned one dollar a day. The same year, O'Keefe purchased the latest in transportation: a 1911 Cadillac. A photograph of the car shows O'Keefe's son, James, seated in the front.

Clearly, Cornelius O'Keefe enjoyed the material benefits of his wealth; however, he did not confine new technology solely to his home. Among other ventures, he financed two movie theatres in

Technology and Other Amenities

James O'Keefe in 1911 Cadillac, ca. 1912.
COURTESY OF THE HISTORIC O'KEEFE RANCH

1911, one in Kamloops and the other in Vernon. The one in Kamloops cost O'Keefe $36,995.21 and was completed in 1913.

The ill-fated *Titanic* played a role in O'Keefe's furniture acquisitions. The Baron and Baroness Herry, principal stakeholders in the Land and Agriculture Company, had booked passage on the fated ocean liner for April 1912. However, Mrs. Herry had strong misgivings about the voyage, so she and her husband changed their reservations and instead arrived on the *Megantic*, with all their belongings intact. After the Herry family fell on hard times, they were forced to sell a number of their possessions to relieve some of their debt load. Never one to overlook an opportunity to acquire fine-quality furniture, even if it were used, and perhaps to help out a business associate, O'Keefe purchased, among other things, a black oak writing desk from them; this desk now stands in the den of the O'Keefe mansion. Were it not for Mrs. Herry's sense of foreboding, O'Keefe would not have had the chance to buy this fine piece.

* * *

O'Keefe continued his involvement with the local Catholic church by again donating land for a new church, this one to be located in the city of Vernon. The congregation had grown considerably since the first Catholic church, St. Ann's, had been built back in 1889 through a subscription initiated by O'Keefe and Mary Ann, on land he had donated. After years of itinerant priests serving St. Ann's, these occasional services were probably not enough to serve the needs of the people of Vernon. O'Keefe and seventeen other area pioneers raised the money needed to construct the new St. James Catholic Church.[4] This church, at thirty metres high, is considerably taller and much more substantial than St. Ann's. Whereas St. Ann's is made of wood, St. James' is made of "rusticated block, dressed to resemble stone."[5]

The erection of this church was O'Keefe's third contribution to a place to worship for the Catholic community, the first being the church on his ranch and the second being the purchase of an organ. Going to St. James' was an improvement upon travelling out to O'Keefe's ranch to attend Mass at St. Ann's. This trip undoubtedly prevented many people from attending church, as a one-way trip from Vernon would have taken an hour by buggy or on horseback, or two and a half hours on foot; the round trip and the Mass together could take up the better part of the day. In

Technology and Other Amenities

winter, the trip would have been an extremely cold one, and in summer, extremely warm, regardless of the mode of travel.

The children of Cornelius O'Keefe would continue in their father's footsteps with their own contributions to St. James'. When Betty O'Keefe, wife of the youngest son, Tierney, died in 1989, her will provided "a memorial gift of padded kneelers." In turn, Tierney requested that memorial donations in his name "be made to the St. James Parking Lot Fund—a project he felt was long overdue and one he had hoped to see completed."[6]

CHAPTER 12

The Beginning of the End

DECLINING PHYSICAL and mental health prevented O'Keefe from enjoying his accomplishments to the fullest. In 1912, he resigned his position as postmaster, a position he had held since 1872. While he and his wife were visiting in Ontario in 1912, he became seriously ill and spent several weeks in the hospital before returning home early in 1913. His health declined further and he suffered from dementia. When he became unable to climb the stairs to the bedroom, Elizabeth converted the main floor den into a bedroom. A devoted wife, she slept on a cot in the same room and stayed with him day and night. About a month before his death, he crawled out of the parlour window and attempted to climb the fence in front of the house, but in the process he fell and injured himself. He died on Monday, March 24, 1919. He was eighty-one years of age.

The Beginning of the End

* * *

Why is Cornelius O'Keefe such an important figure in British Columbia's history? The *Vernon News* said that "O'Keefe's activities were for many years linked up with the progress of the Okanagan... [and that] he became one of the most progressive farmers" in the area. The editorial in the same edition called him "a man of courage, foresight and fortitude." Simply put, he was a forward-thinking entrepreneur who, through hard work and determination, was able to forge a life out of the Wild West. While he was not alone in doing so, he was a colourful and interesting character who left an indelible mark on the ranching industry in British Columbia. He was a leader in many things other than ranching, and his leadership prompted others to engage in similar ventures, thereby helping to increase the economy of the area. He may not have invented new machinery or ranching methods, but he was among the first to try them, providing an example for others to follow.

With great energy and a keen eye on trends in settlement and agriculture, O'Keefe acquired financial success. With greater foresight and imagination than many people of his time possessed—that famous pioneering spirit—he sought out new ideas and techniques not only for his ranching and farming operations, but also for his home. From humble beginnings as the son of an illiterate Irish immigrant, he rose above his family's social and economic position to become one of the most respected pioneers in the Okanagan Valley. The knowledge that he gained in Ontario gave him many of the skills he needed to create a better situation for himself in British Columbia than that which he had left in the east. He carved a place for himself out of British Columbia's wilderness, just as his father had carved his way through the wilds of Ontario. However, what O'Keefe accomplished in British Columbia far surpassed anything that his father accomplished. By any standards, he was a very successful landowner, stock raiser, and farmer; he was equally successful socially, as indicated by his many appointments and elections to various organizations in the Okanagan and Spallumcheen areas. His legacy, which is now known as the Historic O'Keefe Ranch, is one that even he, with his uncanny gift of predicting the future regarding his business, could not possibly have imagined.

* * *

The descendants of the O'Keefe family maintain their interest in their childhood home. They return to the Ranch occasionally; they have attended two family reunions there, the most recent during the summer of 2017 to celebrate the Ranch's one hundred and fiftieth birthday.

CHAPTER

13

The Legacy

AFTER CORNELIUS DIED in 1919, his wife, Elizabeth, continued running the ranching operation, with the help of her youngest son, Tierney, who was born in 1911. She was forced to sell off some of the land to pay back taxes, but she was in ill health herself, and she died in 1929 from Bright's disease. Tierney and his brother, Cornelius Jr., were co-executors of their mother's will. However, at the age of only eighteen years, Tierney was more or less running the ranch on his own.

Between 1929 and the early 1960s, with diminishing income due to market fluctuations and the necessity to pay off further back taxes, the ranch continued to decline. Although Tierney managed to survive the Depression years, his business was not thriving. Like his father before him, he married somewhat late, at the age of thirty-four, in 1945. Apparently, his bride-to-be, Betty Neave, told him that she would not marry him if she had to move into a house without electricity. He must have been extremely serious about marrying her, as he added that particular amenity that same year. They went on to have five children: Eileen, Darcy, Kathleen, Kevin, and Casey. The family persisted in operating the place as a working ranch, raising cattle and producing hay and other feed crops until the early 1960s, when the cattle industry took a further downturn. Now they were faced with the problem of not only having to feed their growing family, but also of what to do with the remaining twenty or so hectares of land—too much land to maintain as a hobby farm, but too small to run as a profitable operation.

According to an O'Keefe family story, the answer came to Betty as she was sleeping. She awoke in the middle of the night with the nugget of a plan in her mind. She woke up her husband, and told him that she had the answer to their problem. The upcoming Canadian centennial, in 1967, gave her the idea that the family should open the ranch to the public and operate it as a heritage site, thereby making it profitable once more. They still had the original church and the log house to which Mary Ann had first come, as well as the mansion where the family currently lived. They would add an addition to the back of the mansion for a new living room, while the existing parlour, den, dining room, and the breakfast room would comprise the heritage portion of the house and would be open to visitors.

Betty's plan was a good one, and the ranch was opened to the public in 1967—a fitting way to celebrate the country's centennial. During the family's tenure as heritage site operators, only the main floor of the house was open to the public; the second floor contained their private rooms. The children remember having to be

The Legacy

very quiet while their father conducted tours. Later, as they grew up, the children took turns conducting visitors through the house. They also remember sliding down the banister in the breakfast room, unbeknownst to their parents! However, none of them sustained a serious fall or required medical attention, unlike their aunt who had done the same thing years earlier. Today, the staircase appears to be green marble. Tierney had painstakingly painted the entire staircase, using a technique called *trompe l'oeil*, French for "fool the eye," replicating the patterns of marble stone.

During the ten years that the family operated the site, many changes were made. One of the first was moving the blacksmith shop from across Highway 97 to the location where it sits today. Originally, it was situated on part of what is now the Spallumcheen Golf Course. In addition, they built a new general store beside the blacksmith shop; both buildings were constructed with lumber taken from other old buildings on the property. Just like in the old days, the general store hosted the post office, where guests could see the various items necessary to the position of postmaster, such as the cancellation stamp for postage. The "new" store is certainly much larger than the original, and it boasts a small wood stove: the only source of heat on cold days. The family also built a boardwalk to join the original log house to the church at the top of the property. This gave visitors a reliable path to follow on their visit.

Tierney O'Keefe and his family wanted their ranch to display items appropriate to the period that the Ranch represents. Many items came from the Ranch, but the O'Keefes also scoured local barns, lofts, estate sales, and auctions, where they found many treasures to furnish the store and other buildings. It was well known among auction-goers that if Tierney O'Keefe was bidding, they might as well give up their own bids, as he always got the items he wanted. Another family story is that the O'Keefe children would use one of these items, the glove sizer, to measure the size of their barn kittens. The hand would go inside a loop, which when tightened would give the hand's glove size.

With their family growing up and moving on to other interests, Betty and Tierney O'Keefe decided to move on. In 1977, they sold the ranch to the now-defunct Devonian Foundation, which in turn donated it to the city of Vernon for use, in perpetuity, as a historic site. After the sale, the second floor was appropriately decorated, and mansion tours included a visit upstairs to see the bedrooms, the schoolroom, and the original indoor plumbing installed in 1910.

All of the local pioneers, including Thomas Wood, A.L. Fortune, Moses Lumby, Price Ellison, E.J. Tronson, and F.G. Vernon, left lasting legacies in the form of schools, villages, parks, residential areas, roads, and cities. Wood lent his name to a lake south of Vernon; Fortune has a creek and a secondary school named in his honour; Lumby has a village that carries his name; Ellison has a provincial park, an elementary school, and an area near Kelowna that all bear his name; Tronson has a road in the Okanagan Landing area; and Vernon has a city that carries his name. As for the Greenhow house, unfortunately, it burned down in 1939. Nothing remains of the original structure except the foundation, upon which a new, much less decorative house was built in the 1940s. This is now the Greenhow Museum.

However, no pioneer left as large a legacy as did Cornelius O'Keefe. His ranch, now the Historic O'Keefe Ranch, is a testament not only to his industriousness but also to the way of life of a

The Legacy

great many people during the latter half of the nineteenth century. The Ranch documents British Columbia's ranching industry and the local history; indeed, it is considered to be the unofficial centre for the history of the ranching industry in the province. It provides a glimpse into a bygone era, when ranching entailed not just wrangling horses but also fine living, with a house that speaks of elegant taste in its original butternut parlour furniture and elaborately carved woodwork. It truly is a step back in time.

Acknowledgements

A WORK SUCH as this is not created by only one person; there are always many people who help the author, and they deserve to be recognized for their contributions, advice, and support.

First of all, to my History 404: History of British Columbia, and History 480: Directed Studies professor, Dr. Duane Thomson: Thank you for encouraging me to take on this project—twice—and to publish it.

To Ken Mather, curator emeritus and former manager of the Historic O'Keefe Ranch: Thank you for all of your help in suggesting sources and for giving me full rein in the Ranch archives, photo files, and the office files. You are a wealth of information!

To Carla-Jean Stokes, curator of the Historic O'Keefe Ranch: Thank you for your editing skills—you pointed out many issues with continuity and flow. Thank you also for providing me with

Acknowledgements

electronic versions of many of the pictures and documents used in this book.

To Barb Bell and the late Ken Ellison, both of the Vernon Museum and Archives: Thank you for your help in searching out various sources, maps, and pictures, and for answering my many questions! A further thank you to Joanne Georgeson, Liz Ellison, and the entire museum staff for your help in finding specific documents.

To the staff in the Ottawa Room of the Ottawa Public Library: Thank you for your help in finding information on the early years of settlement in the Ottawa Valley.

To my cousins, Vern and Ali Armstrong: Thank you for putting up with me for a week and for the use of your car and GPS on my daily drives into Ottawa to do research, and to my cousin, Cari Taylor, who conducted some research for me in Victoria, BC.

To the O'Keefe Ranch itself: Thank you for being such an intriguing subject, and for providing me with endless hours of research, even though at times it was frustrating trying to discover specific information!

To Anne Collinson and retired Okanagan University College history professor Al Hiebert who both read and commented on my manuscript: I appreciate your efforts in helping me improve what I wrote and the way I wrote it.

To Bill Dunsmore, contributor and sometimes-editor of the Okanagan Historical Society: Thank you for reading and making comments on this work; your help was very valuable.

To Hayley Evans, my editor through Heritage House: You have my eternal gratitude for taking on a greenhorn writer and making my work flow. Thanks also for your keen attention to detail!

To Lenore Hietkamp at Heritage House: Thank you for your help in making this book even better. You are a good taskmaster! And finally to my parents, Stan and Mary Field, who have supported me in my endeavours at university and in my current profession as a teacher: Thank you for everything!

Notes

Chapter 2: Humble Beginnings
1. Hugh J.M. Johnston, ed., *The Pacific Province: A History of British Columbia* (Vancouver, BC: Douglas & McIntyre, 1996), 76.
2. Lower Canada was later renamed Québec. Upper Canada became Ontario.
3. Personal Census, 1861, "Ontario Personal Census: Carleton County, Township of Nepean, Enumeration District Number 4," p. 12, lines 28 and 29, microfiche. The census shows that in 1861, Michael and Esther O'Keefe were seventy-six and forty-seven years of age, respectively.
4. Bruce S. Elliott, *The McCabe List: Early Irish in the Ottawa Valley* (Toronto, ON: The Ontario Genealogical Society, 1991), 28, 1–3.
5. Cloth that is "fulled" cloth has been cleaned and thickened by beating.
6. The Canada Company was formed in 1826 to help colonize much of Upper Canada.
7. Bruce S. Elliott, *The City Beyond: A History of Nepean, Birthplace of Canada's Capital, 1792–1990* (Nepean, ON: Tri-Graphic Printing, 1991), 21.

8. Index to Ontario Land Grants—original grants, National Archives, microfiche. The deed for this land was issued in January 1854. Michael O'Keefe acquired this land as a result of the Canada Company plan.
9. H. Beldon & Co, *Illustrated Historical Atlas of the County of Carleton, Including City of Ottawa, Ontario* (Stratford, ON: Cummings Atlas Reprints, 1976; first published 1879), xi.
10. Personal Census, 1861, "Ontario Personal Census," p. 12, line 28.
11. H. Beldon & Co, *Illustrated Historical Atlas*, xi.
12. Harry Walker and Olive Walker, *Carleton Saga* (Ottawa, ON: Runge Press, 1968), 11.
13. Agricultural Census, 1861, "Carleton County, Township of Nepean, Enumeration District Number 4," microfiche, p. 9, line 30.
14. Ibid.
15. Walker and Walker, *Carleton Saga*, 11.
16. Richard Van Vleck, "American Grain Cradles," accessed August 16, 2011, www.americanartifacts.com/smma/grain/cradle/htm.
17. Walker and Walker, *Carleton Saga*, 14, 15.
18. Agricultural Census, 1861, "Carleton County," p. 9, line 30.
19. Ibid., p. 9, line 30 and p. 8, line 29.
20. Personal Census, 1861, "Ontario Personal Census," p. 6, line 44.
21. Ibid., p. 8, line 29.
22. R. Louis Gentilcore, ed., *The Land Transformed, 1800–1891*, Vol. 2 of *Historical Atlas of Canada* (Toronto, ON: University of Toronto Press, 1987), plate 41.
23. Agricultural Census, 1861, "Carleton County," p. 6, line 44.
24. Ibid., p. 8, line 29.
25. Ibid. The carriage was valued at eighty dollars.
26. Personal Census, 1861, "Ontario Personal Census," p. 6, line 44.
27. "Improved land" was that which had been cleared enough to sustain crops or animals, or upon which buildings had been erected. Information on 1842 production is from the Canada West Census, 1842, "Carleton County, Township of Nepean," columns 69–89.
28. Personal Census, 1861, "Ontario Personal Census," p. 4, line 1.
29. Information on 1861 production is from the Agricultural Census, 1861, "Carleton County," p. 8, line 1.

Notes

30. The Tierney robe is embossed with the initials "J.B.T.," indicating ownership by either James or John Tierney. This robe was passed down through the family and eventually made its way to the Historic O'Keefe Ranch where it can be seen in the carriage shed.
31. Ruth Bleasdale, "Class Conflict on the Canals of Upper Canada in the 1840s," in *History 329: Social History of Canada*, vol. 3 of *Book of Readings*, ed. Carol Schafer (Athabasca, AB: Athabasca University, 1990), 225.
32. William N.T. Wylie, "Transience and Poverty: A Study of the Rideau Canal Construction Workers, 1826–1832," in *Rideau Canal Reports, Ontario Region* (Ottawa, ON: Parks Canada, 1981–1982), 29.
33. Walker and Walker, *Carleton Saga*, 117.
34. Ibid., 30.
35. Wylie, "Transience and Poverty," 19.
36. Bleasdale, "Class Conflict," 225.
37. H. Beldon & Co., *Illustrated Historical Atlas*, x.
38. Ibid., xiv.
39. Ibid., xxiii.
40. Ibid., vi.
41. Bruce S. Elliott, *Men of Upper Canada: Militia Nominal Rolls, 1828–1829* (Toronto, ON: The Ontario Genealogical Society, 1995), iii.
42. H. Beldon & Co., *Illustrated Historical Atlas*, xxiii.
43. Ibid., xxxiv.

Chapter 3: Go West, Young Man, Go West!

1. A.R. Buck, "This Remnant of Feudalism: Primogeniture and Political Culture in New South Wales, with some Canadian Comparisons," in *Despotic Dominion: Property Rights in British Settler Societies*, eds. A.R. Buck and Nancy E. Wright (Vancouver, BC: UBC Press, 2005), 17.
2. Thomas Leo O'Keefe, "The Exploits and Adventures of Cornelius O'Keefe, a Pioneer of the Cariboo Mining District, in British Columbia 1862–1867, and the Okanagan Valley 1867–1919," O'Keefe Family Fonds, box 13. Thomas Leo was a son from Cornelius's marriage with Mary Ann.
3. Ken Mather, "O'Keefe, Cornelius," in *Dictionary of Canadian Biography Online*, vol. 14 (University of Toronto/Université Laval, 2003), accessed November 12, 2012, www.biographi.ca/en/bio/o_keefe_cornelius_14E.html.

4. Peter Carstens, *The Queen's People: A Study of Hegemony, Coercion, and Accommodation among the Okanagan of Canada* (Toronto, ON: University of Toronto Press), 70.
5. Mark S. Wade, *The Cariboo Road* (Victoria, BC: The Haunted Bookshop for H.F. Wade, 1979), 32.
6. Ibid.
7. Ibid., 34. Douglas was the governor of the Colonies of Vancouver Island and British Columbia, and he was instrumental in formalizing road building policy in the Cariboo region.
8. Ibid., 57.
9. BC Lands Administration Lists, "Miscellaneous Pre-Emption Records, Lillooet, 1861–62," BC Archives, GR-0985.
10. Wade, *The Cariboo Road*, 53–56.
11. E.O.S. Scholefield and F.W. Howay, *British Columbia: From the Earliest Times to the Present*, vol. 3, *Biographical* (Vancouver, BC: S.J. Clark Publishing Company, 1914), 1068.
12. Wade, *The Cariboo Road*, 84.
13. Ibid., 62.
14. Ibid., 99.
15. Scholefield and Howay, *British Columbia*, 1068.
16. Ibid.
17. Wade, *The Cariboo Road*, 85.
18. Ibid., 88.
19. An eleven-hectare parcel of his original ranch along BX Creek was purchased by Vernon Parks and Recreation in 1994 for use, in perpetuity, as a park, and is now called BX Ranch Park. Nowadays, it is an off-leash dog park, but it is also regularly used by cycling and walking enthusiasts.
20. Art Gray, "Thomas Wood: Pioneer Rancher," ("republished through the kind permission of *The Vernon News*"), in *Thirty-Second Annual Report of the Okanagan Historical Society* (1968), 101.
21. This property is now home to the Vernon Recreation Centre.

Chapter 4: Birth of a Ranching Empire
1. "Land File," O'Keefe Ranch Files.
2. F.W. Laing, *Colonial Farm Settlers on the Mainland of British Columbia, 1858–1871* (Victoria, BC: Provincial Archives, 1939), 460, microfilm. The legal description was "Lot 2, Group 8."

Notes

3. It seems quite probable that the chicken coop was once the O'Keefe cabin, given that the structure has windows that are believed to be original to the building; why would a chicken coop have windows if housing birds was its primary purpose? In 2016, a dendrologist conducted an investigation of the building, but the report has not yet been received by the Historic O'Keefe Ranch.
4. "Land Claims," O'Keefe Ranch Office Files.
5. "Map of Yale District—Osoyoos Div. Tp. 9: Map #52.1," ca. 1887, acc. no. 2002.37.1., Vernon Museum and Archives.
6. Duncan Duane Thomson, *A History of the Okanagan: Indians and Whites in the Settlement Era, 1860–1920* (PhD diss., University of British Columbia, 1985), 272.
7. Ibid.
8. Robert E. Cail, *Land, Man, and the Law: The Disposal of Crown Lands in British Columbia, 1871–1913* (Vancouver, BC: University of British Columbia Press, 1974), 20.
9. Ibid. ("Appendix A: Land Ordinance, 1870," item XXI), 255.
10. "Abstract of Title," transcript of the return of Crown lands sold on the 1877 voters list, p. 9, O'Keefe Ranch Office Files. See also Laing, *Colonial Farm Settlers*, 460. The legal description was "Lot 104, Group 8." In 1876, O'Keefe built his log house on this property.
11. "Land File."
12. Return of Crown Lands Sold on 1880 Voters List," GR-0826, V13, British Columbia Sessional Papers, 1877–1880, 71–75. The legal description reads, "2,648 yards along Okanagan Lake." The certificate was signed by Commissioner William Teague.
13. Photocopy of original indenture, "Lands Conveyed and Dealt with by Cornelius O'Keefe," O'Keefe Ranch Office Files. The land was described as the "south quarter of Section 31, Township 9."
14. "Return of Crown Lands," British Columbia Sessional Papers, 1877–1880, 16. This land later became the subject of a dispute between O'Keefe and the Okanagan Indians who claimed that the land was part of their reserve.
15. British Columbia Surveyor of Taxes, 1876–1958, "Vernon Assessment District, Okanagan, 1876," B400-B453, roll B526, folio 46 (Vernon, BC: Public Archives of British Columbia, 1876).
16. Ibid.

17. Cuyler Page, "Similarities of Several Okanagan/Similkameen Pioneer Flour Mills," in *Fifty-Fifth Annual Report of the Okanagan Historical Society* (1981), 18.
18. Ibid., 22.
19. George Melvin, *The Post Offices of British Columbia, 1858–1970* (Vernon, BC: Wayside Press, 1972), 89. The original spelling of "Okanagon" was changed to the present "Okanagan" in 1905.
20. Robert S. Hall, "Pioneering, as Told to His Daughter, Gladys," in *Nineteenth Annual Report of the Okanagan Historical Society* (1955), 109.
21. Douglas P. Fraser, "From Papers Belonging to His Father, George J. Fraser," Vernon Museum & Archives. Quotations from his father's papers that referred to the time he worked for O'Keefe.
22. Letter, Diocese of Nelson to Catherine O'Keefe, who is married to a great-grandson of Cornelius O'Keefe, "Research File," 3, O'Keefe Ranch Archives.
23. Marriage certificate issued by the office of the Roman Catholic Bishop, Diocese of Kamloops. Translated from the typewritten copy of the records of Immaculate Conception Mission (Pandosy). "O'Keefe Family—Native File," O'Keefe Ranch Archives.
24. "First Family (Mary Ann)," O'Keefe Ranch Office Files. Mary Ann was O'Keefe's first white wife. She wrote of this incident in a letter home to her family in Ontario. Mary Ann's grandniece, Marie Kennedy Lundy, was interviewed by O'Keefe Ranch office manager Diana Martin on July 15, 1987, and told the story.
25. Stuart J. Martin, "Vernon Street Names," in *Thirteenth Annual Report of the Okanagan Historical Society* (1949), 159.
26. H.D. Pritchard and Clarence Fulton, "Story of the Vernon Schools," in *Fifteenth Annual Report of the Okanagan Historical Society* (1951), 137.
27. Jean Barman, "Lost Okanagan: In Search of the First Settler Families," in *Sixtieth Annual Report of the Okanagan Historical Society* (1996), 11.

Chapter 5: The Rancher Finds a Wife

1. M-1954 Fallowfield, Ontario, St. Patrick's Catholic Church (MG9, D 7-63, April 1851–March 1882), 1–248.
2. Union Pacific, "Union Pacific Passenger Trains," accessed August 25, 2012, www.up.com/aboutup/history/passenger_trains/index.htm.

Notes

Chapter 6: Land Disputes

1. Cail, *Land, Man, and the Law* (Appendix A, item xx), 225.
2. Robin Fisher, "An Exercise in Futility: The Joint Commission on Indian Land in British Columbia, 1875–1880," in *Forty-First Annual Report of the Okanagan Historical Society* (1977), 16–17.
3. "Land Claims," O'Keefe Ranch Office Files.
4. Letter, September 10, 1877, "Land Claims."
5. Cail, *Land, Man, and the Law*, 254.
6. Ibid., photocopy. Letter dated September 22, 1877.
7. Sproat to Drake and Jackson, January 20, 1878, "Land Claims."
8. Letters dated September 25 and 28, 1877, respectively, "Land Claims."
9. Cail, *Land, Man, and the Law* (Appendix A), 255.
10. Letter, October 3, 1877, "Okanagan Agency: Correspondence Regarding a Claim to 320 Acres of Land at Okanagan Lake by Mr. O'Keefe (plan)," RG10, volume, 3663, file 9801, Library and Archives Canada.
11. Memorandum dated January 20, 1878, "Okanagan Agency."
12. Ibid.
13. Letter, May 4, 1878, , "Okanagan Agency." O'Keefe had still not removed his property from the land.
14. Letter, April 11, 1879, "Okanagan Agency."
15. Letter, January 31, 1878, "Okanagan Agency."
16. Letter, April 26, 1879, "Okanagan Agency."
17. Chilliheetsa to Sproat, October 5, 1879, "Okanagan Agency."
18. Letter, August 6, 1878, "Okanagan Agency."
19. The 128 hectares in question were eventually turned over to the Okanagan Nation as part of their reserve.
20. Fisher, "An Exercise in Futility," 16–17.

Chapter 7: More Wealth, More Prestige

1. A.J. Hiebert, "District of Okanagan Assessment Roll, 1879," in *Forty-First Annual Report of the Okanagan Historical Society* (1977), 99.
2. Thomson, *A History*, 282–83.
3. "Lands Conveyed," O'Keefe Ranch Office Files (see also the *Sixth Annual Report of the Okanagan Historical Society,* page 184). The land was described as "Lots 38, 62, 65, and 75, Group 1, Osoyoos."
4. Ibid.

5. *Vernon News*, August 21, 1958.
6. Blaine Bovee, "Aquarius 30: The Field of Ardath in Bloom," accessed July 29, 2012, http://sabiansymbol.typepad.com/blain_bovee_sabian_symbol.
7. The Overlanders were a group of about 150 people who left Ontario in 1862; using Red River carts and horses, they travelled to BC to take up new lives.
8. Rosemary Neering, "The First Woman Overlander," *British Columbia Magazine* 45, no. 3 (Fall 2003): 56. Secwepemc is the name of the local Indigenous people in the Shuswap area.
9. *Armstrong Advertiser*, February 28, 1957. The home built by the Schuberts' son is now part of the Historic O'Keefe Ranch. Visitors can go inside and perhaps observe "Mrs. Schubert" baking, ironing, or spinning wool. They can sample baked treats made from old recipes found in the family home and see the spaciousness of the bedroom. The parlour has seen occasional quilting bees staged by local quilters.
10. *Inland Sentinel*, January 17 and February 14, 1884. Long Lake later became Kalamalka Lake.
11. Ibid., April 8, 1886.
12. *Inland Sentinel*, "Notes of Travel," September 11, 1884.
13. Nina G. Woolliams, *Cattle Ranch: The Story of the Douglas Lake Cattle Company* (Vancouver: Douglas & McIntyre, 1979), 44, 79, 46, 58, 63.
14. *Inland Sentinel*, November 9, 1882.
15. Ken Mather, "Visit by the Marquis of Lorne to the Okanagan—1882," in *Fifty-Fourth Annual Report of the Okanagan Historical Society* (1990), 29.
16. Donald Graham, quoted in ibid.
17. Ibid., 27.
18. Mrs. William Brent, "The Priest's Valley School: Some Okanagan Valley Dates," in *Seventeenth Annual Report of the Okanagan Historical Society* (1953), 114.
19. *Vernon News*, Oct. 26, 1893.
20. "Moses Lumby," Vernon Museum and Archives.
21. *Vernon News*, Oct. 26, 1893.
22. Margaret Ormsby, "A.L. Fortune's Autobiography," in *Fifteenth Annual Report of the Okanagan Historical Society* (1951), 26.
23. Beverley Howlett, "Alexander Leslie Fortune—Okanagan Pioneer," people file "A.L. Fortune," Vernon Museum and Archives.

Notes

24. *Inland Sentinel,* March 20, 1884.
25. "Notes of Travel," *Inland Sentinel,* September 11, 1884.
26. Martin, "Vernon Street Names," 159.

Chapter 8: Additions, Achievements, and Accolades

1. Deaths 1885-1939, Images: 1885-2014, "Births, Deaths, Marriages," Vernon Museum and Archives.
2. "Okanagan Correspondence," *The Victoria Daily Colonist,* August 12, 1888.
3. This method involves drilling holes and carving dowels to fit, and it uses no nails. The staircase is still strong today.
4. Elliott, *The City Beyond,* 61.
5. Walker and Walker, *Carleton Saga,* 143-44.
6. Elliott, *The City Beyond,* 62.
7. "Church File," O'Keefe Ranch Office Files. A copy of the subscription list is posted on the wall in the church.
8. Gaston Carrière (OMI, CM, Archivist, Archives Deschâtelets) to O'Keefe Ranch researcher Jocelyn Van Overbeek, August 15, 1982, "Church File," O'Keefe Ranch Office Files.
9. "Vernon Museum," O'Keefe Ranch Office Files.
10. *Vernon News,* June 18, 1891.
11. Ibid., June 23, 1898.
12. Ibid., February 17, 1897.
13. David Mitchell and Dennis Duffy, eds., *Bright Sunshine and a Brand New Country: Recollections of the Okanagan Valley, 1890-1914,* vol. 8, no. 3 of Sound Heritage (Victoria, BC: Provincial Archives of British Columbia, 1979), 9.
14. *Vernon News,* October 15, 1891.
15. Ibid., October 29, 1895.
16. Ibid., August 4, 1898; R.M. Middleton, ed., *The Journal of Lady Aberdeen: The Okanagan Valley in the Nineties* (Victoria, BC: Morris Publishing, 1986), 83.
17. Middleton, *The Journal of Lady Aberdeen,* 80, 14.
18. *Vernon News,* November 26, 1896.
19. Ibid., December 23, 1897.

Chapter 9: Cattle Baron to Land Baron

1. Bill dated July 25, 1897, pre-1889 file, Box 1 (1887–1914), O'Keefe Ranch Office Files.
2. Ibid., photocopy of original order.
3. Michael Hagan, *Inland Sentinel*, December 7, 1889.
4. *Vernon News*, May [?]; August 6; October 1, 1891.
5. *Inland Sentinel*, December 5, 1891.
6. Thomson, *A History*, 264.
7. Receipt for purchase of cow and calf from J.T. Steele, Box 1: 1887–1914, pre-1889 file.
8. Woolliams, *Cattle Ranch*, 31.
9. *Inland Sentinel*, February 23, 1889.
10. Ibid., December 7, 1889, and April 6, 1889. The organizational meeting had been held in March, 1889, and was reported in *Inland Sentinel* on April 6.
11. Ibid., December 7, 1889.
12. Ibid.
13. Cowboy Showcase, *Reading and Understanding Livestock Brands*, accessed January 4, 2013, www.cowboyshowcase.com.
14. "Brands," Vernon Museum and Archives.
15. Cowboy Showcase, *Reading and Understanding*.
16. Ibid. Branding remains the best way to prove ownership, but the methods have changed with new technology. These days, ranchers can microchip their animals—including ostriches, llamas, bison, and other "exotic" creatures—or use a laser-type brand that destroys the pigmentation in the hair so that the brand appears white. Most owners of premium stock also have detailed photographs of their animals, showing variations in colour and locations of distinctive markings, as well as written descriptions of these same telltale marks.
17. Hagan, *Inland Sentinel*, May 23, 1889.
18. *Vernon News*, June 18, 1891.
19. Thomas Stevenson, "An Old-Timers Celebration," in *Ninth Annual Report of the Okanagan Historical Society* (1941), 52–53.
20. *Vernon News*, April 12, 1894.
21. *Inland Sentinel*, October 9, 1888. The property was on the east side of the arm of Okanagan Lake, situated in Township 13.

Notes

22. Ibid., November 17, 1888. This land was the south half of Section 35, Township 13.
23. *Inland Sentinel,* May 11, 1889. A chain is twenty metres, so the first acreage had almost 1,219 feet of lake frontage and the second over 762 metres along the lake. Eighty chains equals 1.6 kilometres.
24. Leonard Norris, "The First Steamboat on Okanagan Lake," in *Sixth Annual Report of the Okanagan Historical Society* (1935), 260–61.
25. Receipt from the school, file 1889, Box 1, 1887–1914, O'Keefe Family Archives.
26. *Vernon News,* March 2, 1905; January 4, 1906.
27. *Inland Sentinel,* February 8, 1890.
28. *Vernon News,* July 2, 1891. The purchase included the north half of Section 31, Township 9, and the south half of Section 6, Township 8. Thomas Greenhow had died in 1889, leaving his widow in charge of his estate.
29. Ibid., October 1, 1891.
30. Ibid., January 22, 1892. The land was described as the fractional part of the east half of Section 15, Township 8.
31. Photocopy of indenture, dated February 1, 1892, "Lands Conveyed." O'Keefe paid $127 for the land described as "the west half of Lot G7."
32. *Vernon News,* January 28, 1892; March 5, 1892.
33. Ibid., March 24, 1892; March 10, 1892. "Commonage" refers to the land that was used by several ranchers for pasturage purposes.
34. Ibid., March 23, 1893; September 8, 1892.
35. Ibid., May 18, 1893.
36. Ibid., June 2 and 23, 1892; April 6, 1893.
37. Ibid., October 15, 1891.
38. Ibid., October 12, 1893; October 11, 1894.
39. *Vernon News,* September 24, 1896.
40. Obituary, *Vernon News,* bid., September 26, 1940.
41. *Vernon News,* October 12, 1893; Michael Hagan, "A Trip Through the Okanagan Valley in 1888," in *Sixteenth Annual Okanagan Historical Society Sixteenth Annual Report* (1952) 19.
42. Transcript in "Elizabeth File," O'Keefe Family Archives.
43. *Vernon News,* June 3, 1892.
44. R.B. Bell and R.O. Constant, "A Few Okanagan Homes" (Vernon, BC), Vernon Museum and Archives.

45. *Vernon News*, March 19, 1896.
46. Elizabeth went on to finance her daughter's house, which was torn down in 1974 to accommodate what is now the Vernon Lodge Hotel.
47. Edgehill Manor was a care home for physically and mentally challenged adults, but it is now a private residence once more.
48. People file "R.B. Bell," Vernon Museum and Archives. This home was later purchased by the Mackie family, who operated the Vernon Preparatory School for Boys. Now called the Mackie Lake House, it is used for weddings and other events, including Victorian teas and an artist retreat.
49. Flora M. Cooper, "Mr. and Mrs. R.B. Bell, Pioneer Residents of Vernon," in *Fifteenth Annual Report of the Okanagan Historical Society* (1951), 193.
50. R.B. Bell, "The Story of My Life: 1850 to Christmas 1936," People file, "R.B. Bell."
51. This story was told, somewhat gleefully, to Ken Mather (curator emeritus of the O'Keefe Ranch) by Mary while she was on a visit to the Ranch with her sister, Margaret. Mather reports that while Mary took great delight in telling the story, Margaret was quite silent.
52. Hagan, "A Trip," 19.
53. *Vernon News*, November 16, 1893.
54. Ibid., May 9, 1895.
55. Mitchell and Duffy, eds., *Bright Sunshine*, 9.
56. Fraser, "Papers Belonging to His Father."
57. Ibid.
58. Mitchell and Duffy, eds., *Bright Sunshine*, 9.
59. Fraser, "Papers Belonging to His Father."
60. Mitchell and Duffy, eds., *Bright Sunshine*, 9.
61. "Cornelius O'Keefe Charged with Assault" (July 1897), 34–35 (police court record), Vernon Museum and Archives.
62. Fraser, "Papers Belonging to His Father." A "whiffletree," as defined by *Merriam-Webster*, is "the pivoted swinging bar to which the traces of a harness are fastened and by which a vehicle or implement is drawn."
63. Leonard Norris, "Humour in the Okanagan," in *First Annual Report of the Okanagan Historical Society* (1926), 27–28.
64. Ibid.
65. *Vernon News*, April 12, 1894; July 27, 1893; July 12, 1894.

Notes

66. "Price Ellison Fonds: 1884–1966," MS-0007, 98208-5, *MemoryBC*, memorybc.ca; accessed July 3, 2012.
67. J.B. Kerr, *Biographical Dictionary of Well-Known British Columbians* (Vancouver: Kerr & Begg, 1890), 160.
68. Ken Ellison, "A Short History of an Okanagan Valley Pioneer" (1988), 11. Privately published.
69. Ellen Ellison Sovereign, "A Tribute to my Father," *Vernon News*, August 16, 1962.
70. Nellie Tutt, *History of Ellison District, 1858–1958* (Kelowna, BC: Ellison Centennial Committee), 7. The Chinook language was a pidgin trade language—a combination of several Indigenous languages, English, and French.
71. Ellison, "A Short History," 38.
72. *British Columbia Gazette*, November 2, 1893.
73. *Vernon News*, September 16, 1897.
74. Hagan, *Inland Sentinel*, December 5, 1891.
75. *Vernon News*, March 24; June 16; December 8; December 15, 1892.
76. Original bill from Nicholles and Renouf, February 24, 1894, file "1891-1899," Box 1 (1887–1914), O'Keefe Ranch Archives.
77. *Vernon News*, March 22, 1894.
78. File "1891–1899," Box 1 (1887–1914), O'Keefe Ranch Archives.
79. James E. Jamieson, "Donald Graham... Early North Okanagan Pioneer," in *Thirty-Eighth Report of the Okanagan Historical Society* (1974), 12–13.
80. "Town and District," *Vernon News*, March 28, 1895.
81. Photocopy of original indenture, April 1, 1896, "Lands Conveyed."
82. Ibid., photocopy of indenture, dated April 8, 1896.
83. *Vernon News*, August 20, 1891.

Chapter 10: Marriage, Mining, and Milling

1. One child died as an infant in 1882.
2. *Vernon News*, February 2, 1889.
3. Ibid.
4. Jo Jones, ed., *Hobnobbing with a Countess: The Diaries of Alice Barrett Parke* (Vancouver: UBC Press, 2001), 128. Her diary entry is dated February 2, 1899.

5. *Vernon News*, February 2, 1899.
6. Elliott, *The City Beyond*, 47.
7. Ibid., 73.
8. Both the cutlery and the chest are on display in the dining room of the mansion.
9. *Vernon News*, June 26, 1902.
10. Richard Wolfenden, "Annual Report of the Minister of Mines for the Year Ending 31st December, 1899," in Vernon Museum and Archives (1900), 188.
11. A mineral claim is similar to a gold claim, but in addition to gold, other minerals such as copper, silver, or lead are sometimes found.
12. *Vernon News*, February 4, 1897.
13. Ibid., March 8, 1897.
14. *Vernon News*, February 26, 1896.
15. Box 4, O'Keefe Family Archives.
16. "Map #1441," accession no. 967.091.001 (1907), Vernon Museum and Archives.
17. The "mansion," the original log house, the church, and other buildings remained in the family until 1977, when the remaining twenty hectares with all the buildings were sold to the Devonian Foundation, which then donated the entire site to the City of Vernon as a heritage site.

Chapter 11: Technology and Other Amenities

1. *Vernon News*, December 29, 1910.
2. Ibid.
3. This boiler still heats the house today, although it was converted from coal-burning to natural gas. To see the house now, one would never guess that this particular feature was not original to the time of construction.
4. Canada's Historic Places, "St. James Catholic Church," *Parks Canada*, accessed March 4, 2018, www.historicplaces.ca/en/rep-reg/place-lieu.aspx?id=17105.
5. Ibid.
6. Kathleen O'Keefe-Nield, "Tribute to Tierney O'Keefe, 1911–2000," in *Sixty-Fifth Annual Report of the Okanagan Historical Society* (2001), 164–66.

Bibliography

Archival Sources

O'Keefe Archives
Box 1, 1887–1914, file "1889"; Box 4; "Elizabeth File." O'Keefe Family Archives.

Box 1, 1887–1914, files "pre-1889," "1890," "1891–1899"; Box 1A; "O'Keefe Family—Native"; "Photo Files"; "Research File." O'Keefe Ranch Archives.

"Church"; "First Family (Mary Ann)"; "Land Acquisition and Occupation"; "Land Claims"; "Land File"; "Land Records: Cornleius O'Keefe"; "Land: Original Pre-emption: Lot 2, Group 8"; "Lands Conveyed and Dealt with by Cornelius O'Keefe"; "Pre-1889"; "Research"; "Vernon Museum." O'Keefe Ranch Office Files.

O'Keefe, Thomas Leo. "The Exploits and Adventures of Cornelius O'Keefe, a Pioneer of the Cariboo Mining District, in British Columbia 1862–1867, and the Okanagan Valley 1867–1919," box 13. O'Keefe Family Fonds.

Other
Miscellaneous Pre-Emption Records, Lillooet, 1861–62. GR-0985, BC Lands Administration Lists. BC Archives.

"Okanagan Agency: Correspondence Regarding a Claim to 320 Acres of Land at Okanagan Lake by Mr. O'Keefe (plan)," 1877–1889. RG10, volume 3663, file 9801. Microfilm. Library and Archives Canada.

Record of Baptisms, St. James Parish, 1900. Diocese of Kamloops.

Vernon Museum and Archives

Files: "Brands"; "A.L. Fortune"; "Moses Lumby"; "R.B. Bell"; "Douglas P. Fraser."

"Births, Deaths, Marriages." Images: 1885–2014. Master/DEATHS/Deaths 1885–1939. Microfilm.

"Cornelius O'Keefe Charged with Assault" (July 1897), 34–35. Police court record.

"Map: Subdivisions of Estates in the Vicinity of the City of Vernon." Compiled by Mutrie & Mutrie.Acc. no. 967.091.001.

"Map of Yale District—Osoyoos Div. Tp. 9: Map #52.1," ca 1887. Acc. no. 2002.37.1.

Published Sources

Agricultural Census, 1861. "Ontario Agricultural Census: Carleton County, Township of Nepean, Enumeration District Number 4." Microfiche.

Barman, Jean. "Lost Okanagan: In Search of the First Settler Families." In *Okanagan History: The Sixtieth Annual Report of the Okanagan Historical Society*, 8–20. Vernon, BC, 1996.

BC Legislative Assembly. "Annual Report of the Minister of Mines for the Year Ending 31st December, 1899." Victoria, BC: Queen's Printer, 1900.

Bleasdale, Ruth. "Class Conflict on the Canals of Upper Canada in the 1840s." In *History 329: Social History of Canada*. Vol. 3 of *Book of Readings*, ed. Carol Shafer, 225–57. Athabasca, AB: Athabasca University, 1990.

Brent, William (Mrs.). "The Priest's Valley School: Some Okanagan Valley Dates." In *Seventeenth Annual Report of the Okanagan Historical Society*, 112–115. Vernon, BC, 1953.

Buck, A.R. "This Remnant of Feudalism: Primogeniture and Political Culture in New South Wales, with some Canadian Comparisons." In *Despotic Dominion: Property Rights in British Settler Societies*, ed. A.R. Buck and Nancy E. Wright. Vancouver: University of British Columbia Press, 2005.

Cail, Robert E. *Land, Man, and the Law: The Disposal of Crown Lands in*

Bibliography

British Columbia, 1871–1913. Vancouver: University of British Columbia Press, 1974.

Canada West Census, 1842. "Carleton County, Township of Nepean."

Carstens, Peter. *The Queen's People: A Study of Hegemony, Coercion, and Accommodation among the Okanagan of Canada.* Toronto, ON: University of Toronto Press, 1991.

Cooper, Flora M. "Mr. and Mrs. R.B. Bell, Pioneer Residents of Vernon." In *Fifteenth Annual Report of the Okanagan Historical Society*, 191–94. Vernon, BC,: 1951.

Elliott, Bruce S. *Men of Upper Canada: Militia Nominal Rolls, 1828–1829.* Toronto, ON: The Ontario Genealogical Society, 1995.

———. *The City Beyond: A History of Nepean, Birthplace of Canada's Capital, 1792–1990.* Nepean, ON: Tri-Graphic Printing, 1991.

———. *The McCabe List: Early Irish in the Ottawa Valley.* Toronto, ON: The Ontario Genealogical Society, 2002.

Ellison, Ken. *Price Ellison: A Short History of an Okanagan Valley Pioneer.* Oyama, BC: K.V. Ellison, 1988. Privately published.

Fisher, Robin. "An Exercise in Futility: The Joint Commission on Indian Land in British Columbia, 1875–1880." In *Forty-First Annual Report of the Okanagan Historical Society*, 8–22. Vernon, BC, 1977.

Gentilcore, R. Louis, ed. *The Land Transformed, 1800–1891.* Vol. 2 of *Historical Atlas of Canada.* Toronto, ON: University of Toronto Press, 1987.

Gray, Art. "Thomas Wood: Pioneer Rancher." In *Thirty-Second Annual Report of the Okanagan Historical Society*, 99–104. Vernon, BC, 1968.

Hagan, Michael. "A Trip Through the Okanagan Valley in 1888." In *Sixteenth Annual Report of the Okanagan Historical Society*, 15–36. Vernon, BC, 1949.

Hall, Robert S. "Pioneering, as Told to His Daughter, Gladys." In *Sixteenth Annual Report of the Okanagan Historical Society*, 15–36. Vernon, BC, 1955.

Hiebert, A.J. "District of Okanagan Assessment Roll, 1879." In *Forty-First Annual Report of the Okanagan Historical Society*, 97–99. Vernon, BC, 1977.

Illustrated Historical Atlas of the County of Carleton, Including City of Ottawa, Ontario. Stratford, ON: Cummings Atlas Reprints, 1976. Reprint of the 1879 edition published by H. Belden & Co., Toronto.

Jamieson, James E. "Donald Graham... Early North Okanagan Pioneer."
In *Thirty-Eighth Annual Report of the Okanagan Historical Society*,
11–13. Vernon, BC, 1974.

Johnston, Hugh J.M., ed. *The Pacific Province: A History of British Columbia*.
Vancouver, BC: Douglas & McIntyre, 1996.

Jones, Jo, ed. *Hobnobbing with a Countess, and Other Okanagan Adventures:
The Diaries of Alice Barrett Parke, 1891–1900*. Vancouver, BC: UBC
Press, 2001.

Kerr, J.B. *Biographical Dictionary of Well-Known British Columbians*.
Vancouver, BC: Kerr & Begg, 1890.

Laing, F.W. *Colonial Farm Settlers on the Mainland of British Columbia,
1858–1871: With a Historical Sketch by F.W. Laing, Secretary to the Minister
of Agriculture, 1916–1937*. Victoria, BC: BC Provincial Archives, 1939.
Microfilm.

Martin, Stuart J. "Vernon Street Names." In *Thirteenth Annual Report of
the Okanagan Historical Society*, 156–61. Vernon, BC, 1949.

Mather, Ken. "O'Keefe, Cornelius." In *Dictionary of Canadian Biography
Online*, vol. 14. University of Toronto/Université Laval (2003). Accessed
November 12, 2012. www.biographi.ca/en/bio/o_keefe_cornelius_
14E.html.

———. "Visit by the Marquis of Lorne to the Okanagan—1882." In *Fifty-
Forth Annual Report of the Okanagan Historical Society*, 24–29.
Vernon, BC, 1990.

Melvin, George. *The Post Offices of British Columbia, 1858–1970*. Vernon:
Wayside Press, 1972.

MemoryBC. "Price Ellison Fonds: 1884–1966." MS-0007; 98208-5.
Memorybc.ca.

Middleton, R.M., ed. *The Journal of Lady Aberdeen: The Okanagan Valley
in the Nineties*. Victoria, BC: Morris Publishing, 1986.

Mitchell, David, and Dennis Duffy. *Bright Sunshine and a Brand New Country:
Recollections of the Okanagan Valley, 1890–1914*. Sound Heritage Series,
vol. 8, no. 3. Victoria, BC: Provincial Archives of British Columbia, 1979.

Neering, Rosemary. "The First Woman Overlander." *British Columbia
Magazine* 45, no. 3 (Fall 2003): 56–57.

Norris, Leonard. "Humour in the Okanagan." In *First Annual Report of the
Okanagan Historical Society*, 27–28. Vernon, BC, 1926.

Bibliography

———. "The First Steamboat on Okanagan Lake." In *Sixth Annual Report of the Okanagan Historical Society*, 260–62. Vernon, BC, 1935.

O'Keefe-Nield, Kathleen. "Tribute to Tierney O'Keefe, 1911–2000." In *Sixty-Fifth Annual Report of the Okanagan Historical Society*, 164–66. Vernon, BC, 2001.

Ormsby, Margaret. "A.L. Fortune's Autobiography." In *Fifteenth Annual Report of the Okanagan Historical Society*, 25–40. Vernon, BC, 1951.

———. "A Study of the Okanagan Valley." Master's thesis. Vancouver: University of British Columbia Press, 1931.

Page, Cuyler. "Similarities of Several Okanagan/Similkameen Pioneer Flour Mills." In *Fifty-Fifth Annual Report of the Okanagan Historical Society*, 18–23. Vernon, BC, 1981.

Personal Census, 1861. "Ontario Personal Census: Carleton County, Township of Nepean, Enumeration District Number 4."

Pritchard, H.D., and Clarence Fulton: "Story of the Vernon Schools." In *Fifteenth Annual Report of the Okanagan Historical Society*, 137–43. Vernon, BC, 1951.

"Return of Crown Lands Sold on 1880 Voters List." GR-0826, V13, 71–75. Department of Lands and Works (1871–1908). British Columbia Sessional Papers, 1877–1880.

Scholefield, E.O.S., and F.W. Howay. *British Columbia: From the Earliest Times to the Present*. Vol. 3, *Biographical*. Vancouver, BC: S.J. Clarke Publishing Company, 1914.

Stevenson, Thomas. "An Old-Timers Celebration." In *Ninth Annual Report of the Okanagan Historical Society*, 52–55. Vernon, BC, 1941.

Thomson, Duncan Duane. *A History of the Okanagan: Indians and Whites in the Settlement Era, 1860–1920*. Vancouver: University of British Columbia Press, 1985.

Tutt, Nellie. *The History of Ellison District, 1858–1958*. Kelowna, BC: Ellison Centennial Committee, 1959.

"Vernon Assessment District, Okanagan, 1876." B400–B543, roll B526, folio 46. British Columbia Surveyor of Taxes, 1876–1948, Public Archives of British Columbia, Vernon, BC.

Wade, Mark S. *The Cariboo Road*. Victoria, BC: The Haunted Bookshop for H.F. Wade, 1979.

Walker, Harry James William, and Olive Walker. *Carleton Saga*. Ottawa, ON: Runge Press, 1968.

Woolliams, Nina. *Cattle Ranch: The Story of the Douglas Lake Cattle Company*. Vancouver, BC: Douglas & McIntyre, 1978.

Wylie, N.T. William. "Transience and Poverty: A Study of the Rideau Canal Construction Workers, 1826–1832." In *Rideau Canal Reports, Ontario Region*. (Ottawa: Parks Canada, 1981–1982), 19–29. Microfiche Report Series.

Index

Aberdeen, Countess of, 67, 68
Aberdeen, Lord, 68, 95
Ashcroft, 45

Barkerville, 9, 29
Barman, Jean, 40
Barnard, Francis Jones, 28, 29, 30
Baudre, Father I.M., 48
Bazile and Aleck, 48
Bell, R.B., 81, 83–86
Big Bend, 30, 59
Boucherie, I., 89
Brent, Frederick, 89
British Columbia Cattle Association (BCCA), 2, 71–72, 74
BX Ranch, the, 28, 30, 98

Bytown, 11, 21, 23, 65
Bytown and Prescott Railway, 23

Cameron, W.F., 88, 99
Canada Company, the, 12
Cape Horn, 44
Cariboo (goldfields), 6, 7, 9, 29
Cariboo Gold Rush, the, 9
Cariboo Wagon Road, the, 9, 27–28
Carleton County, 11–13
Carleton Saga (book), 13
Carlyle, W.A., 102
Cascade Mountains, 35
Chilliheetsa, Chief, 50
Christine, 38–39
Clark, A., 103

Coldstream Ranch, 36, 52, 54, 79, 95
Columbia Milling Company, 69, 95
Constant, R.O., 84, 85
Cortez, Hernando, 73
Crozier, James, 89
Cumming, Captain, 99

Deep Creek, 33, 36, 81
District of Yale. *See* Yale
Dontonville, Bishop of New Westminster, 67
Douglas, Governor James, 27
Drake and Jackson, 48, 50
Durien, Bishop of New Westminster, 66, 101

1851 Census of the Township of Nepean in Carleton County, 12, 22
1842 Census for Canada West—Carleton County, 11, 12
1861 Personal Census for Carleton County, 13, 15
Ellis, Thomas, 88, 89
Ellis, W.E., 102
Ellison, Price, 52, 54, 66, 73, 75, 80, 93–94
Enderby, 54, 59

Fallowfield, 11, 23, 65
Fisher, Robin, 51

Fortune, A.L., 52, 54, 59, 89, 99, 118
Fraser, George J., 38, 88, 90, 91
Fuller, A.G., 102, 103

Girod, Philip, 49
Girouard, Luc, 30, 74, 78, 88, 89
Greaves, J.B., 56, 79, 96
Greenhow, Elizabeth,
  cattle sales, 96
  donations to church, 65, 66
  land ownership, 55, 78
  new home construction, 81–83, 85
  wife of Thomas, 31
  Women's National Council, 67, 101
Greenhow, Thomas,
  cattle rancher, 30, 52, 74
  death, 31, 66
  entrepreneur, 76–77
  land acquisition, 32
  land sales, 35, 74–75, 105
  partnership with O'Keefe, 47–47, 55
  tragedy, 63

Hagan, Michael, 55, 60, 64, 70, 71, 74, 87, 94, 95
Hall, Robert S., 37
Harris, Isaac, 38, 39
Head of the Lake, 94, 103
Henderson, G.A., 99

Index

Herry, Baron and Baroness, 109
Holliday, C.W., 40
Houghton, Charles Frederick, 52, 53, 54

Isthmus of Panama, 27

Land and Agriculture Company, 106, 109
Land Ordinance of 1870, 34-35, 46
Lequime, Bernard, 89
Lequime, Eli, 66
Lorne, Marquis of, 56-59
Lower Canada, 11
Lumby, Moses, 59, 88, 89, 118

Mason, H.S., 76, 96
Mather, Ken, 5
McKenna, Charles, 16, 17, 18, 20
McLean, Stan, 5
McMicking, Thomas, 54
McMullen, A.J., 102, 103
Megaw, W.E., 85

Nepean, 12-13, 18, 20, 23-24, 65
Neave, Catherine, 90
1902 Minister of Mines Report, 102

Okanagan Flour Milling Company Limited, 70, 103

Okanagan Flouring Mills Company, 1, 96
Okanagan and Spallumcheen Agricultural Society, 2, 74, 80, 92
O'Keefe, Betty (née Neave), 111, 115-16, 118
O'Keefe, Charles, 100, 107
O'Keefe, Cornelius,
   BCCA member, 71-72
   cattle brands, 73-74
   cattle buyer, 30-31, 34, 56, 71-72, 74, 79
   employer, 88-91
   grain farmer, 69-70, 95
   grist mill, 1, 36
   house renovations, 62, 64-65, 81-85, 107-8
   land acquisition, 32-33, 35-36, 52-53, 55, 77, 78, 96
   land disputes, 46-51
   land sales, 96, 104, 106
   marriages, 38-42, 99-100
   militia, 23, 60-61
   mining, 101-3
   moving west, 26-28
   obituary, 6-7
   Okanagan and Spallumcheen Agricultural Society member, 80-81, 92
   Okanagan Flour Milling Company, 103

Ontario, 10, 14–15, 21–22, 65
orchardist, 94
politics, 93–94
postmaster, 37, 112
St. Ann's Catholic Church, 65–67, 110
St. James Catholic Church, 110
stock raiser, 79
tragedy, 63, 107
Vernon Jockey Club, 2, 92
O'Keefe, Cornelius Jr., 77, 115
O'Keefe, Eileen Sr., 77
O'Keefe, Elizabeth (née Tierney), 18, 73, 77, 99–101, 112, 115
O'Keefe, James, 108, 109
O'Keefe, Leo, 5, 77
O'Keefe, Lillie, 77
O'Keefe, Margaret, 77, 86, 87
O'Keefe, Mary, 86
O'Keefe, Mary Ann (née McKenna)
  death, 98
  hostess, 57–58, 63, 66–67, 86
  marriage, 41–42
  moving west, 43–45
O'Keefe, Michael and Esther (née Esthère Demers or Esther Demara), 11–14, 18, 19–22, 24
O'Keefe, Nellie, 77
O'Keefe, Tierney, 83, 90, 111, 115–16, 117–18
  children, 116, 118

Oram, Edna, 5

Parke, Alice Barrett, 98
Perry, Evan, 102
Polson, Samuel, 104

Rideau Canal, the 11, 22
Robertson, William, 28
Robinson, Honourable Peter, 11
Rosie, 37–40, 41
  a.k.a. Alapetsa, 38
  a.k.a. Rosa, 38
Royal Engineers, 9

Saint Lawrence Canal, 11, 22
Schubert, Augustus, 52, 54
Shaw, Charlie, 88, 90
Sicamous, 74, 93
Soda Creek, 45
Spallumcheen, 32, 49, 114, 117
Spinks, William Ward, 96
Sproat, Gilbert, 47–51
Steele, J.T., 79
Swan Lake, 35, 76, 78–79, 96, 104

Tierney, Denis, 18–20, 65, 99
Tierney, James, 65, 99
Tierney, John, 19, 20
Tierneys, the, 16, 18

Index

Tronson, E.J., 40, 66, 74, 75, 88, 89, 91, 94, 99, 118
Vernon, C.A., 47, 73, 91
Vernon, Forbes George, 52, 74, 91, 118
Vernon Jockey Club, 92

Walker, Harry and Olive, 13
Welland Canal, 22

Wells Fargo, 29
Winfield (Lake Country), 30
Women's National Council, 67, 101
Wood Lake, 30
Wood, Thomas, 30, 73, 74, 118

Yale, 38–39

About the Author

SHERRI FIELD'S interest in the life of Cornelius O'Keefe began when she was a student at Okanagan University College and continued for the four years that she worked as heritage interpreter at the Historic O'Keefe Ranch. Her fascination with O'Keefe led to years of research into his long and prolific life, and eventually to this book. When she is not writing, Field teaches high school English in Enderby, BC.